Dimensions of Development Practice

Dimensions of Development Practice

Uma Joshi

Sonia Bendre

AUTHORSPRESS

Worldwide Circulation through Authorspress Global Network
First Published 2010
by
Authorspress
E-35/103, Jawahar Park
Laxmi Nagar, Delhi-110 092
e-mail: authorspress@yahoo.com

Dimensions of Development Practice
ISBN 978-81-7273-505-0

Printed in India at Tarun Offset, Delhi.

Preface

Development practitioners are the heart of any development programme. In the twenty-first century development is conceived with new dimensions in all its aspects. It puts emphasis on qualitative improvement in human life with new indicators, approaches and sustainability of development. Thus, it requires trained and competent professionals to handle the process of development. Therefore, development practice is emerging as a profession, and development practitioners are seen as agents of change.

As a result, many universities have started courses on "Development Management". However, there is a dearth of research in this area. To strengthen the training and preparation of development practitioners, studies on development practitioners' perceptions to their practices should receive attention of the development training institutes. This book throws light on one such study focusing on perceptions of development practitioners regarding the selected aspects of development.

The book can help in planning curriculum and learning experiences for development management students in a more meaningful way. The book will also provide insight to the NGOs in providing inputs for enriching the development practitioners to put their best efforts in the development work.

Prof. Uma Joshi

Sonia Bendre

Contents

1

Concept of Development

Development is the goal of every nation, and various strategies are being planned to achieve development, encompassing all spheres of life—political, economic, social and spiritual. Today it is more than ever the common goal of mankind. Its purpose is to build an enabling environment so that people can enjoy a long, healthy and creative life. In the last six decades, scholars have proposed various theories and models, and some of these theories have failed to yield results, and new theories that emerged have tried to offer solutions to speed up the development. The term 'development' has been interpreted in various ways by sociologists, economists, development planners and so on.

Therefore, with the usage, the meanings of development have multiplied and have kept on increasing in scope. The content and meaning of development has always taken several forms. So ordinarily, development refers to a process whereby latent potentialities of an object/organism unfold and manifest incrementally. This object's/organism's intrinsic capabilities are realised so that its mature form may be attained. Once the object /organism achieves this full-fledged state, it/he may be said to be developed (Trivedi, 1998).

Since development is viewed as social change, Rogers (1976), an influential scholar, described development as "a widely participatory process of directed social change in a society, intended to bring about both social and material advancement including greater equality, freedom and other valued qualities for the majority of the people through their gaining greater control over their environment" (cited in Murthy, 2006).

Development has become a global "civil religion" during the past more than 40 years—a battle cry for all nations – rich or poor, strong or weak. It is a complex revolutionary process—more a process of social change rather than merely generation and accumulation of economic resources. Development thinking has evolved into a broad spectrum realisation that it must move beyond economic growth to include important social goals—reduced poverty, improved quality of life, and enhanced opportunities for better education and health and more.

Development has been defined in various ways. The Indian Institute of Mass Communication defined development as the removal of poverty, the lessening of disparity between regions and classes, the building up of technological infrastructure, modernisation of society through shedding feudalism, tribalism and superstitions, and the gradual achievement of economic self-reliance (Ganesh, 1994: 83).

Development means sustainable economic growth combined with human development. The United Nations Development Programme (UNDP) and the United Nations (UN) organisations are also guided basically by this concept.

According to Lee, "development is a process for acquiring a sustained growth of system's capability to cope up with the new, continuous changes towards the achievement of progressive political, economic and social objectives" (cited in Joshi, 2001).

Cairrcross (1995) has defined development as "not just a matter of having plenty of money, nor it is purely economic phenomenon. It embraces all aspects of social behavior, the establishment of law and order, the relationships between family, literacy and scrupulousness in business dealings and familiarity with mechanical gadgets" (Gupta, 1995: 62).

Development is the prime inexorable force of the human condition. It is not just restricted to the mere upliftment of the economic status of a nation, but involves a whole gamut of issues pertinent to the well being of a group of individuals and the society at large. Man is defined by development since development is the only means man possesses to fulfil his potentiality, ensure his self-esteem, secure his view of a good life and realises to self. What man is and what man attains is because of development. Development is presented with messianic reverence as the panacea for mankind's socio-economic and political ills. It is seen as the key to individual and collective peace, progress and prosperity. It is perceived as a state which promises a solution to the most intractable. Because of all that it promises, development has become the single most important objective of the individual and of the state. (Trivedi, 1998)

Edwards (1999) has defined development in part as "an increased opportunity for vulnerable being: the reduction of material want and the enhancement of people's ability to live a life they consider good across the broadest range possible in a population." (In Gasper : 44-45)

Todaro (2000) has defined development as a complex of social and cultural attitudes and economic changes for which one should strive for the fulfilment of basic needs of the people. He said that "Development must be conceived as a multidimensional process evolving major changes in social structure, popular attitudes and national institutions as well as the acceleration of economic growth and eradication of poverty. Development must be turned to the basic needs and desires of individuals or social groups." (62)

Wang and Dissanayake (1984) defined development as "a process of social change which has as its goal the improvement in the quality of life of all or the majority of the people without doing violence to the natural and cultural environment in which they exist and which seeks to involve majority of the people as closely as possible in this enterprise, making them masters of their own destiny." (5)

Thus development can be defined as the improvement in the human life condition at individual and societal levels which is achieved through desirable but fluctuating changes or adjustments in the environment.

Some interpret development as attainment of number of modernisation ideals such as rise in productivity, social and economic equalisation, modern knowledge and improved institutions and attitudes. Development is cherished by all individuals, communities and nations, irrespective of their culture, religion and spatial location. It should not uproot people from their culture and environment but it should help them to become self-sufficient and self-reliant. Development as a discipline and profession is not just concerned with development planning that prioritises development sectors or development policy goals but more importantly with the need for a cross-sectoral, people-centred approach to development.

Development is thus seen as a pluridimensional concept. This fact is reflected in the abuse of the adjectives that accompany the word "development" – economic, social, political, cultural, sustainable, finally human to mention a few. It is the sum total of allround balanced and planned growth.

1.1 History of Development in India

For a majority of us, development seems imminent and inevitable. The journey of development started a long way back and is still continuing, and will probably never come to an end, as it is a continuous process. The only thing that is constant is change. Development came to be universally defined as natural, beneficial and inevitable. The meaning and significance of development went through a number of ups and downs.

The story of free India has so much drama, intrigue, joy and sorrow that it can put our best movies in the shade. India and Pakistan came into existence as independent nations in August 1947, bathed in the blood of communal butchery. If freedom was tempered by the horrors of partition, the progress India made in every decade was accompanied by conflicts and tensions (Prakash, 2007 :17).

After independence, development work was found in the form of adult educator, extension worker or community worker, and so on. The theoretical explorations began to appear in the form of teaching of extension education, adult education and so on. This viewed people working for community and development as the change agents. They aimed at helping, guiding and educating people within local community to identify social needs, to consider the most effective ways of meeting there and to set about doing so, in so far as their available resources permit. The terms 'community development' and 'extension education' became popular in the early period of independence in India.

Later the term 'community development' spread much wider with the changed parameters and indicators of development at national and international levels. It emphasised on taking account of the interrelation between different services available and their accessibility, needs of people, deciding ways of meeting the needs of the people and development challenges arising out of constantly changing society and environment and inter-agency coordination, planning and policy formulation. Thus working for development of communities and societies has become a crucial and challenging task. This requires professional training and practice in development work to bring about social change. It cannot be done through a part-time social or development work. It is a full-time professional task.

Immediately after independence, development strategy in India was concerned with the issue of 'growth with stability'. In the post-independence period due to colonial hangover and the urgent need to catch up with the west the model which defined development in economic terms was adopted. Development was equated with economic growth manifested in ever rising Gross Domestic Product (GDP) and measured against quantifiable parameters. It implicitly acknowledged that the quantitative outlook of the West was more conducive to development that indigenous beliefs and values were often characterised as 'other worldly'.

The decade of the fifties opened with India's future direction in limbo. In this decade, gravest of all was the economic situation: the effects of Partition, which disrupted economic networks and created a large refugee population, were now superimposed upon endemic poverty. Economic growth was synonymous with development. But this period saw some fundamental accomplishments. Most foundational were the consolidation of the state and its assertion of sovereignty over the social. Law was established as a basic tool for India's self-transformation. The second defining impulse was the will to create institutions, from the Atomic Energy and Planning Commission to the Election Commission. Third, the state secured a subcontinent as a zone of relative peace with conditions of economic stability under a democratic government (Khilnani, 2007). Another milestone in our attempt for overall development was the introduction of the five-year plans. Each plan had its thrust area. Agriculture was the highest priority for the first five-year plan that was expected to bring the whole of India – agricultural, industrial, social and economic – into one framework of thinking.

The things that did not happen in the 1950s were equally consequential. Firstly, the government failed to educate the citizenry. A second missed opportunity was the inability to alter Indian's unequal distribution of land ownership.

Two distinct theories emerged in the fifties, namely, the Modernisation theory and the Dependency theory. The essence of the modernisation theory was the transfer of Western technology and rationality, without changing class structure as a means of development and removal of all social and ideological obstacles to such a process (Alavi and Shanin, 1982: 13). It envisages that development can be achieved only through industrialisation, urbanisation and westernisation along with technological transformation of agriculture.

Till the 1960s, dominant paradigm guided intellectual thinking influencing development theory. It stressed economic growth through industrialisation, capital-intensive and machine-intensive technology, a top-down structure of authority with economists in charge and a certain attitude and mindset among individuals. This industrialisation was the focus of the second five-year plan. Rise in per capita income was considered as an important indicator for development in terms of education and culture. The concept of overall development of society of the fifties, widely known as community development which aimed at the development of the entire population, was shifted in the mid-sixties to understand development, specifically of the poor. The dominated development, policy saw direct links between growth and development and the emphasis was more on production rather than distribution. Development was seen as a linear process and equated with industrial growth, modernisation and liberal democracy. This decade also witnessed the launch of two of India's leading financial dailies, *The Economic Times* and *The Financial Times*. The late 1960s saw the Green Revolution, which brought a major technical and socio-economic transformation. Soon self-sufficiency in food production was achieved. The characteristics of Green Revolution are intensive irrigation, profuse use of chemical fertilisers, pesticides and electrical energy.

From seventies, however, the development concept was refined and broadened through the addition of first, the ecological dimensions – population, food, employment, human sentiment and lately science and technology including technology transfer. The early concern for 'growth with stability' was shifted in the seventies to 'growth with social justice'. Issues of distribution and equity came to the forefront. The failure of the growth model to make major inroads into poverty and unemployment led to a shift from growth to basic needs, income distribution and employment generation as the prerequisites of poverty alleviation. It pointed out that another development is geared to the satisfaction of basic needs – it is endogenous and self-reliant, in harmony with the environment, and requires structural transformations. The non-economic concepts such as distributive justice and equality of life as measured by social indicators like life expectancy, nutritional levels, education, physical quality of life and many more entered the development paradigm.

Thus the concept of service extension has broadened to include economic development, community practice and capacity building. The approaches included centrally planned initiatives rather than just community organisation and development.

At present, the development work is supposed to strengthen the ability of community organisations and various groups of people in building their structures, systems, people and skills so that they are better able to define and achieve their objectives, participate in planning and implementing the development programmes and become partners in development. This requires development practitioner to move ahead of the concept of extension service and community organisations.

The development practices in India have been reoriented once again since the mid-eighties to associate the notion of empowerment with 'development'. Empowering people, particularly women, to strengthen their capacities was the main objective of development and its principle resource. This reorientation aimed at ensuring the basic necessities of life to the people 'by sharing power' with them through institutionalised means, i.e., laws, legal procedures and international obligations. The significant point of departure here is that while the earlier discourses saw the poor people as 'beneficiaries', the emergent one has recognised them as 'partners of development'. Accordingly there has been a new coinage of the term 'human development' since the mid-eighties with the recognition that the 'human person is the central subject of development'. The context of this reorientation, however, has been globalisation and the structural adjustment programme that implicitly or explicitly looks for the reduction of state expenditure in the social sector – health, education, food security and other basic needs and the encouragement of privatisation. Thus the state emerged as 'central to economic and social development not as a direct provider of growth, but as a partner, catalyst and facilitator' (World Bank, 1997). This reflected a change in the philosophy of developmentalism. The eighties, termed as a lost decade, also witnessed deepening economic crisis and debt situation which ultimately culminated in the development discourse, such as gender, environment, sustainable development and people centred development. The concepts of 'sustainable development' or people centred development marked a shift in development theory and practice.

In the nineties, however, the milieu was one of 'economics in command'. Growth of production and modernisation of technology and management were supposed to be the central goals of development in the contemporary wave of the structural adjustment programme. Liberalisation and privatisation of the economy, and its integration with the global economy have been advocated essentially on the grounds of development production. India reaped the benefits of liberalisation but the threat of imbalanced growth remained to be addressed. Mainstream development was increasingly caught by the horns of a dilemma between the aims of human and social development, and the constraints of structural adjustment and global monetarism represented by international financial institutions.

1.2 Development in India—Present Scenario

Over the past few decades a major shift seems to have taken place in the concept of development. People's attention is an essential prerequisite of empowerment process. Thus the redefined concept of development indicated new goals for participative development in the third world countries like:

- Equity in distribution of benefits of development which placed emphasis on the poorest of the poor, those living in backward rural areas and urban slums.

- Active participation of the people at the grassroots.
- Reliance on local human skills and material resources thus fostering greater self-reliance in development and importantly leading to freedom from external agency.

Thus people became the focus of development and of them the poor majority. There was a shift from linear approach to a multidimensional approach.

Fifty years of development experience have yielded four critical lessons: First, microeconomic stability is an essential pre-requisite for achieving the growth needed for development. Second, growth does not trickle down; development must address human needs directly. Third, no one policy will trigger development; a comprehensive approach is needed. Fourth, institutions matter; sustained development should be rooted in processes that are socially inclusive and responsive to changing circumstances.

These challenges must be confronted even as many forces reshape the development terrain: innovations in technology, the spread of knowledge, the growth of population and its concentration in cities, the financial integration of the world and rising demands for political and human rights.

There was a need for fundamentally different alternative development paradigm – that puts people at the centre of development, regards economic growth as a means and not an end, protects the life opportunities of future generations as well as the present generation and respects the natural systems on which all life depends. Sustainable development represents an important alternative paradigm to the economic/market paradigm generally adopted by World Bank. Such a paradigm of development enables all individuals to enlarge their human capabilities to the full and to put those capabilities to their best use in all fields – economic, social, cultural and political. Alternative development has been concerned with alternative practices of development—participatory and people-centred—and with redefining the goals of development. Mainstream development has gradually been moving away from the preoccupation with economic growth toward a people-centred definition of development.

The alternative paradigm is a fundamental reinterpretation of the current development conceptions. According to this paradigm, development means creating a sustainable society that fulfills basic need of human beings, where the relationship between the society and nature is non exploitative. It is the vision of a peaceful society. The World Commission of Environment and Development (WCED) and the Brundtland Commission (1987) defined Sustainable Development as that which meets the needs of the present without compromising the ability of the future generations to meet their own needs. Sustainable development requires meeting the basic needs of all and extending to all the opportunity of satisfying their aspirations for a better life. It implies a new concept of economic growth – one which provides fairness and equal opportunity for all, not the privileged few, without further destroying world's finite natural resources and without compromising the world's carrying capacity.

In the twenty-first century the principal goal of development policy is to create sustainable improvements in the quality of life for all people. While raising per capita incomes and consumption is part of that goal, other objectives—reducing poverty, expanding access to health services and increasing educational levels—are also important. Two main forces to shape the world in which the development policy was to be defined and implemented: Globalisation (The continuous integration of the countries of the world) and Localisation (The desire for self-determination and the devolution of power).

At the beginning of the twenty-first century, the concept of development has undergone a radical change. Cambridge (2002) stated that at present, development is recognised as complex, integral, participatory process involving stakeholders and beneficiaries and aimed at improving the overall quality of human life through improvements in a range of social sectors in an environmentally responsible manner (Murthy, 2006:5).

In 2000, at the United Nations Millennium Summit, 189 member nations came together to make the elimination of poverty and the fulfilment of human rights their highest priorities. From this, path-breaking agreement was born the Millennium Development Goals (MDGs) – eight objectives to accelerate human development, achieve universal equality and attain a more peaceful world by 2015. The world in 2015 will be one of our own making: a reflection of our shared success or failure – to meet the goals and ensure that all people have the means to fulfil their individual potential. It has generally been accepted that achieving sustainable development will require balancing environmental, societal, and economic considerations in the pursuit of development and an improved quality of life. Thus, sustainable development aims to promote harmony among human beings and between humanity and nature.

This decade saw a number of ups and downs. There was rapid industrialisation, urbanisation and globalisation. The technological advancement has reached heights with a boom in the Information Technology (IT). Women's empowerment is of major concern with the women conquering different fields.

Awareness regarding development programmes must be an integral part of all development policies and programmes and this means an emphasis on development sensitive policy formulation and implementation. A task-oriented approach to development is reflected in the ubiquity of logical framework planning and its variants, in which development interventions are planned on the basis of devising a logic by which tasks or activities will lead to desired outcomes and thence to the achievement of set goals. This task requires an effective and efficient management. Thus the concept of development management emerged.

The growing development sector needs trained professionals. Working for development sector requires a set of qualification, skills, competencies, values and attitudes. Beyond skills and expertise, what is especially important is an identification with the values that we believe in which include a drive towards striving for excellence and working and thriving in diversity.

Although the development sector is booming in India, many challenges are still to be overcome and problems are to be solved.

1.3 Development Management

Development management encompasses "the management of intervention aimed at external social goals in a context of value-based conflict". Intervention in this sense means influencing social processes, rather than using resources to meet goals directly. External social goals are achieved by actions in the public sphere, directed outside a given organisation rather than internal to it. Since individual social actors seldom have more than partial control over a given development process, value based conflict is an intrinsic part of development management.

Development management is more about dealing with the messiness of intervening for change, with the importance of feelings and intuitions, with uncertainty and risk taking, with handling conflict and diversity with mutual respect, with what is not said and is not visible that it is about establishing concrete facts and objectively verifiable indicators, quantifying achievements or seeking to put reality, into neat packages labelled 'projects'. Development management is, then, concerned not with exercising control or counting beans, but with seeking to act on as understanding of how change processes intersect with power, and of how best to shape those processes in favour of those who are excluded from resources and decision making.

Development management is a growing discipline that aims to refine development through its concern for national and global diversity. It aims at creating responsible, self-reliant and resource-based communities capable for developing and implementing activities in a manner consistent with the principles of people empowerment where the development practitioners play a vital role.

2

Development Practitioners

There are many problems existing in the Indian society. For carrying out the development work, national and international agencies are there to provide the funds. But it is necessary to bring those funds to the field and carry out the development work. The development practitioners are the channels through which one can reach the grassroots level people. It is very difficult to bring about a social change than any other kind of change because it involves new orientation to the habits, customs, traditions, values and motivation of individuals and alternations in several social institutions. The development practitioners are the key persons who can bring change in attitudes and behaviour of the people. They are considered the opinion moulders in the community (Ojha, 1983:8).

Development practice is based on the belief that people can participate in purposeful development activity and give direction to their future. How this becomes possible is based on the characteristics of the participating community and people, their issues and their resources. Today, development means gaining knowledge and empowerment through a process of collaboration and action. It provides for experiences through which people become responsible and concerned for their situation, and decide and implement plans of action.

Development practitioners work on the assumptions that behavioural change can be brought about among people through interaction and giving purposeful direction to their behaviour and they are capable of participating in the process of their development. Thus development practice is based on the belief that maximising purposeful interaction and dialogue within a community will increase the potential for learning and development.

Up to the 1960s extension education described development work. It meant working with people and communities to make them strong and more aware and enlightened. It aimed at extending agency's activities and services to the community. Following the major social and economic changes after independence, slowly development work under extension became more and more professionalised. Society was facing new challenges of the twenty-first century which required more deliberate programme framework and specialised training in development work. In the modern process of development and social change development practice is a necessary full-time professional task.

Earlier development was equated with economic growth through industrialisation. Development programmes were planned and imposed by sociologists and economists. Extension workers, educators and functionaries played an important role during that era. They followed the orders given by the higher authority. Their role was to inform and aware people about their basic needs and interests. The programmes of development did not show any positive impact as people were considered the objects of development.

Over the years, with experience and condition of the society, the role of extension educators started taking a different shape. They started working with the people for long hours. In the process they built up sufficient rapport and enjoyed a distinct credibility to communicate and convince families for positive change. Their role was to help the people identify their felt needs and to assist them in meeting the needs with the available resources. They also disseminated knowledge to bring a desirable change in the knowledge, skill and attitudes of the people. Today, the extension educators, social workers are looked upon as development practitioners. They learn a variety of useful entrepreneurial skills such as how to stay organised, how to manage people, strong sense of ethics and problem solving skills, as well as an ability to build collaborations and partnerships between various organisations. It is very important for them to be aware of the programmes and policies of development and its major objectives. They play a crucial role in changing the lifestyle of the people. They act as change agents, inventing new approaches and creating new solutions to change society for the better. They come up with new solutions to social problems and then implement them on large scale.

Today, the development sector in India is growing and expanding providing numerous employment opportunities. It also contributes to the development of the society. According to Chanchalapathi Dasa, vice chairman, The Akshaya Patra Foundation, "the Indian social sector is booming and currently, it is going at a phenomenal speed and its time for people to consider a career in the social sector as a very viable option."

Although it is considered a passion rather than a profession to be involved in social work, like other sectors development sector also needs professionalism in its management so as to make it more efficient in resource utilisation as well as goal and result-oriented. In India, development sector is focusing on development of downtrodden, marginalised, weaker and vulnerable sections of society.

Government, non-government, voluntary agencies as well as corporate sectors are all involved in development work at various levels. These have opened a wide range of employment opportunities in development sector. Thus, the development sector, which is also known as social sector, has become one of the leading sectors in our country providing employment opportunities to those who aspire and believe in making difference.

The primary mission of the development practitioner's profession is to develop and empower the people of deprived groups. They have to lead the society towards equality and justice by educating people to participate in ending dissemination, oppression and inequalities. To achieve these objectives, development practitioners have involved themselves in direct contact with people, organisation of communities, supervision and monitoring of development activities, promoting social and political action for development and policy formulation and implementation. Development practitioner's work is rooted in certain values such as willingness to serve society, integrity, respect for humanity and so on. They are also required to have a code of ethics which provide guideline for effective development practice. These are required irrespective of the group or setting or programmes they work. Code of ethics serves many purposes, such as providing ethical standards of development practice and identifying the relevant solutions and considerations when any conflict or questions related to ethics in development practice arise. Code also keeps a practitioner aware of the principles, values and standards to follow through out their development work.

Development sector faces the biggest challenge of sustaining development practitioners, paying lucrative salaries and employing trained professionals. Many NGOs are not able to pay salaries comparable to the corporate sectors. However, corporate sectors taking up social responsibility are able to pay higher and offer many other perks and benefits. This motivates the ambitious person with passion for development work to remain in development sector and work for a cause.

The development sector is growing at a faster rate. Development practitioners from government, non-government organisations, corporate sectors, freelancers and so on are joining the development sector. Corporate sectors are traditionally known for profit making in terms of high returns and contribute to the economic development. Today they are expected to expand their boundaries by involving themselves in taking up social responsibility. It is an applied concept. The emphasis of development organisations has shifted from top-down approach to participatory and interventions approach.

They are expected to be professional, experienced in planning, implementing and managing development programmes at various levels. Their work is not just restricted to planning, executing and supervising development programmes, but they are required to document the reports. Thus, they are required to have various competencies to solve the problems of the people and face the challenges that come in the way. They are expected to play facilitative role in development. Their role has become far more challenging and complicated now.

The need for more formal education and training in development work was felt to strike a balance between the rapid changes occurring across the country and coping with the development needs arising out of it. It was felt necessary that those practising development have basic knowledge and skills in the processes, and methods of development work. Thus, to make the country's development efforts more potent and strong, the need for well articulated development framework was inevitable. Thus, extension education professionals were brought into broader concept of development work which focused on development issues at national as well as regional and local levels, preparation of development professionals and more professional approach to the development process. Here, the term 'development' is broader than just economic development or industrial development. It also includes the components like housing, education, recreation, social organisations, leadership development, self-reliance, gender equality, health and so on.

Two approaches are generally found to be applied in development work. One is practice-based approach. Here development practitioners develop their own personalised theories based on their field experiences and practice in development. Their actions, behaviours, thinking, strategies, confidence in development practice are influenced by their field experiences.

Secondly, the practitioners' assessment of community using data from various sources of information, their interaction with key groups and leaders helps them to decide the strategy for development work in a particular community. Thus, the development practice has not been explored from models or paradigms point of view. This is because the situations and groups with which development practitioners work are so complex and specific that standardising any models of practice may not be possible. Their practice is situation specific, and practitioners have to refine it continually; they have to prepare their strategy for new projects and situations based on the values and beliefs they have derived from their past field experiences.

A development practitioner's work has three major aspects. First, to educate and help people to identify their needs and problems and take action on the specific issues which are of great concern or importance to them. This may involve finding, generating, redistributing and utilising resources for development. Secondly, to make political leaders realise their responsibility for development of the society. This requires dialogues, meetings and involving them in decision making and planning development project. Thirdly, in the present context of communal sensitivity, development practitioners face the challenge of maintaining communal harmony wherever they are involved in development work, especially areas known as communally sensitive.

Development practitioners have to promote active participation of people in problem identification, decision making of the project as it affects their life. They have to suggest alternative solutions to the problem. They have to work towards increasing leadership capacity of the target group. It involves developing or upgrading skills and knowledge, confidence building and raising aspirations.

Over the last two decades it has become increasingly clear that a pre-occupation with defining development in pre-dominantly economic terms has frequently resulted in policies and programmes that have produced negative social outcomes, especially for poor men and work.

Development practice as a profession and an area of study is not just concerned with development planning which focuses primarily on social policy goals but more importantly with the need for a cross-sectoral people-centred approach to development. Development practice is a growing discipline that aims to refine development through its concerns for national and global diversity and social justice in order to better ensure development outcomes that are contextually sensitive, socially accountable and equitable.

All the development programmes and policies should aim at improved well being and dignity of all individual men and women.

Education for development practice should have the major objective of developing critical, analytical and practical skills in its practitioners. Development practitioners should be able to work with people at their own level and to find common ground. They may not believe in what people do or agree with them but they need to have compassion and the commitment to understand them and to support them as they learn to participate in the development process. Thus human rights and dignity should be the basic frame of reference for development practitioners. They should use culturally appropriate and sensitive approaches to promote development and protect human rights. Development practitioners should be able to tolerate ambiguity, individual differences and inflexible attitude on the part of the people participating in development. They should have the willingness to help others develop skills and knowledge, the commitment to the development of their target group, excellent written and verbal communication skills, planning and organising skills and so on.

The term *community work* or *development work* has a relatively short history.

Education for development practice is now an integral part of the development strategy for any country. Earlier the community work was not conceived beyond the narrow objectives of problems and needs of communities or raising political awareness. Now, the concept of development is seen as an educational process, creating opportunities for growth and change, increasing their knowledge, skills, awareness and change attitudes. The empowerment of communities and individuals is seen as one of the major aims of development work today.

There are five areas which education for development practice should encompass. These are:

- *Professionalism:* The development practitioners must possess the required knowledge and subject matter as well as skills for working effectively and competently.
- *Planning and implementation:* Development practitioners must have an indepth understanding of the process of planning and implementing development programmes, and the ability to interpret the indicators of success and failure of the programme.
- *Communication:* Communication skills, both oral and written, the ability to communicate with both professional as well as target groups, community leaders, funding agencies and with government bodies are of utmost importance.
- *Team work:* Development work requires team work at various levels as it is multidisciplinary and

multidimensional work. Thus development practitioners require good interpersonal skills enabling and facilitating their work.

– *Orientation of target group:* To find out appropriate solutions for development related problems and seek people's participation in development process, it is very important that the practitioners have orientation of their target groups. Planning and implementation cannot be done without the orientation of the target group. (Total.com)

2.1 Theoretical Limitations for Development Practitioners

Theories of development and development practice are based on the theories of various disciplines from social sciences. Thus, it requires multidisciplinary approach and becomes a challenging task for development practitioners to evolve one of their own. Every discipline has its academic boundaries, approaches and philosophy. Moreover, the development has to have local perspective to be effective in its outcomes. Thus, it becomes difficult for a development practitioner or a researcher to decide what is important for community development practice or research. For example, development practice requires knowledge of management, sociology, communication development process and its theories, extension education research methods and so on.

Development practice has to adjust to the new contexts continuously and occupational settings. There are uncertainties related to stable funding to the agency and stability of development profession. Whatever may be the uncertainties in development practice, the profession is growing overwhelmingly. Many a time, communities are not able to make distinctions among paid development practitioners, activists, voluntary development workers, and relationship between them. Many practitioners conclude that the theories of development are inapplicable in day-to-day development practice.

3

Perceptions of Development Practitioners – A Study

Development has become a common goal of mankind. It is absolute, inevitable and universal, promoted as a laudable goal, no matter what the society, the culture, the people and their resources and traditions. The present study will focus on the perceptions of development practitioners in the present context of development.

With the paradigm shifts, today's era has seen rapid change in the concept of development. The digital revolution in the twenty-first century has brought a new dimension for visualising development, its concepts, indicators, approaches and so on. The concept of development has changed from merely economic growth to improvement in human life condition. The linear approach is shifted to a multidimensional approach.

Development is now measured in Human Development Index (HDI) and not only in Gross Domestic Product (GDP). Human development is the process of both quantitative change and qualitative growth. There is a shift from the earlier thrust of quantitative to the qualitative improvement of human life. At present India ranks 127th in the Human Development Index (HDI) which is very low. To change the qualitative life of the people better development inputs are required. These inputs can be better if the development practitioners are competent. To make the training inputs effective for development practitioners, it is necessary to know how the present context of development is perceived by the development practitioners, as the extent of clarity of the concept of development leads to meaningful planning and implementation of development work.

Though a number of massive development programmes have been initiated, there is less of satisfactory change in this direction and lot more requires to be done. Seventy per cent of the population of India resides in rural areas. There are wide-ranging target groups and content areas to be catered to in the rural areas. Special target groups require special approaches. Although technological advancements have played a major role in rural development, there is little change in the lives of the people at the grassroots level. Secondly, the major problems in the country namely illiteracy, poverty, unemployment, population explosion, low health status and many more have remained unsolved. Exploring the perceptions of development practitioners will help in knowing as to what are the problems in attaining the results of the development work.

Many efforts in the form of programmes and policies are made for the development of the country. Development has become a dire need for the citizens of the country. It involves long-term objectives as sustainable development has become important. Only trained professionals can be competent to handle such projects or programmes. Development practice is emerging as a growing profession. Development practitioners have become important agents of development. The variety of content areas requires skills in their treatment.

Various types of divides such as economic divide, digital divide, communal divide, information divide and so on are emerging, so development requires efficient handling, fund raising, and its management, utilisation and documentation skills. This requires competent professionals and practice of development with a professional approach. Research is a requirement for training activities of development practitioners and provides guidelines for developing such training. Therefore, studying the development practitioners' perceptions can go a long way in planning training strategies for them.

Development is an emerging area of study. It is exploratory in nature. However, there have been reports of development programmes and projects conducted by government and non-government organisations, etc. but hardly any systematic study is found on development as perceived by the development practitioners.

Development research is primarily aimed at development practitioners. The new concepts of development, its approaches, priority areas of concern, competencies required for development practice, problems in development work and challenges are already recorded by scholars in books, but how these are perceived by those practising development need to be studied. The study will help in generating knowledge which can be transformed into practice. This will help in making development programmes more meaningful and effective. Thus, the study on perceptions of development practitioners regarding the selected aspects of development was felt justified.

The perceptions of development practitioners regarding development would help the curriculum planners to better understand the concept of development and its aspects as understood by the practitioners. This would help them to plan the curriculum and learning experiences for the students in a more meaningful and functional way. Findings of the study would help the teachers to select more relevant learning experiences and strengthen their training in development management.

The findings of the study would develop understanding among the development practitioners, extension workers, educators and social workers about how the development practitioners perceive development in the present context and what more is needed to be done about training practitioners.

The study would throw light on the approaches for planning development programmes, competencies required by the development practitioners in doing development work and the priority areas of concern for development. This would help teachers and planners to select appropriate approaches and build up the required competencies for development work.

Therefore, it was decided to conduct a study on the perceptions of development practitioners regarding the selected aspects of development.

3.1 Statement of the Problem

In the light of the above discussion, the following questions were raised:

- How do development practitioners perceive development in the present context?
- What problems and challenges do they face in practising development?
- What are the thrust areas in practising development?
- What are the competencies required by development practitioners to carry out development work?
- Are development practitioners able to utilise the present indicators and approaches for development?

To seek answers to these questions it was decided to take up a study on the perceptions of development practitioners regarding the selected aspects of development.

3.2 Significance of Research on Development Practitioners

Research on development provides relevant information and analysis about people's needs, demands and receptivity for development inputs. Development practitioners are directly involved in planning and executing programmes at the grassroots level. They are aware about different situations at the grassroots level. They are the change agents and the link between people and planners. This link has to be strong and effective. So to study the perceptions regarding development, the development practitioners could be the best source to gain insight into how they perceive what they are professionally engaged in.

Development practitioners may vary in their background. They are at the nucleus of development management as they are directly involved with the people at the grassroots level. Their clarity with the concepts of various aspects of development is very important for effective implementation, and effective monitoring and evaluation of development programmes. The present study will throw light on the areas of development management that require training and concept clarification on the part of the development practitioners through training. It will help in revising, modifying and strengthening the academic inputs for the development practitioners.

Apart from this, the people at the grassroots level are close to the development practitioners. They put all their demands, needs and problems in front of the practitioners. Therefore, clarity in perceptions of the development practitioners can help them to plan and execute better programmes, apart from establishing rapport with them and involving them in development process.

The study will throw light on the competencies required by the development practitioners, the problems faced in development practice and the challenges in development work. This will serve as an extremely useful resource for training and equipping development practitioners with the skills for effective development practice in the context of needs of people and community. It will also be of interest to the curriculum planners for development management training, non-government organisations, government agencies and corporate sectors as well as funding agencies. They can work out the ways in which the development practice can more adequately respond to the perceptions of its practitioners, their competencies and the problems they face.

Studies have been conducted on specific groups such as non-formal educators, adult educators and extension educators. These studies are on specific programmes and their aspects. But hardly any study is conducted on development practitioners in the present context of development management. Thus, selecting the sample of the development practitioners for the present study was justified.

3.3 Objectives of the Study

1. To study the perceptions of development practitioners regarding the following selected aspects of development:
   a) Concept of development
   b) Priority areas of concern for development
   c) Approaches to development
   d) Competencies required by development practitioners
   e) Problems in development work
   f) Challenges for development practitioners
2. To study the overall differences in the perceptions of development practitioners regarding the problems

in development work in relation to the following variables:

a) Concept of development
b) Priority areas of concern for development
c) Approaches to development
d) Competencies required by development practitioners
e) Problems in development work
f) Challenges for development practitioners

3.4 Delimitations of the Study

1. The study was delimited to the selected aspects of 'development', i.e., the concept of development management, approaches, priority areas, competencies required by development practitioners, problems and challenges.
2. The study was delimited to the development practitioners from the State of Gujarat.

3.5 Operational Definition

Development Practitioners – In the present study the term 'development practitioners' means the individuals who are involved in practising development for improving the human life conditions at individual and societal level to create responsible and self-reliant communities, and who are employed in development organisations or practising development freelance.

3.6 Variables of the Study

An individual reacts differently to different situations or circumstances due to possession of different personal characteristics like aggressiveness, extrovert, emotional. The development practitioners may also differ from each other. Differences in personal characteristics may affect their perceptual process and show differences in their perceptions. Thus, it was felt important to study whether such individual difference also show difference in their perceptions. Therefore, the independent variables were selected for the study and perceptions of the development practitioners were treated as dependent variable.

1. *Age:* Growth in age is inevitable. It is the most important factor, which affects the lifestyle of an individual. Researchers have scientifically proven that young age group is more alert, enthusiastic and active. They are risk takers and full of spirit. They tend to be highly ambitious but less experienced. They may perceive economic growth as an essential indicator to development. Younger generations may have received specialised training in development as development has emerged as discipline recently. On the other hand, the older age group may have set ideas and experience in their approaches, more protective, more realistic and more conservative. They may have their own established facts and perceptions for development and its concept. Therefore it was decided to take age as one of the variables of study.
2. *Sex:* Sex is one of the most important aspects of one's individuality. Males and females differ in their psychology. Due to the differences which males and females display, they have considerable disparity in their interests, attitudes, thoughts and feelings.

Due to the differences in the brain of boys and girls, they show differences in the interest, feelings, attitudes and thoughts. Males are realistic and tough by nature. Females are sensitive and emotional by nature. Generally both are differently brought up. Their socialisation process is usually different. Therefore males and females may visualise world and thus development with a different perspective. Thus it was considered important to take sex as a variable of study.

3.7 Educational Qualification's

Education expands the boundaries of life and clears vision towards one's goals and objectives of life. It Education sharpens the qualities of a human being.

With higher educational qualification, more knowledge, finer thinking and specificity about related knowledge are expected. With education the analytical and evaluative competencies develop. Those who are less educated may have developed limited thinking and ability to comprehend. Apart from this, what kind of qualification helps to build clear perception of development management can also be found out by studying this variable.

Therefore, educational qualification was taken as one of the variables of study.

3.8 Types of Organisations

There are various types of organisations engaged in development practice. These organisations work with their own approaches and perspectives. Each organisation has its own way of working, funding resource, target groups, areas of concern and priorities. The development practitioners may vary in their perceptions according to the type of development organisation.

The non-government organisations are dedicated to people's development and are fully involved in development practice. Their resources and structures of planning and implementing development programmes also differ. Therefore, it was of interest to find out whether the type of organisation of development practitioner makes any difference in their perceptions on the selected aspects of development or not.

3.9 Length of Experience in Development Work

Experience can be a vital factor in training the perceptions of the development practitioners. It helps the individual in many ways. More experienced practitioners may have developed a deeper understanding and vision in their work. They may have some proven and established practices and ideas. They may have more knowledge of development work. Therefore they may perceive development practice in a different perspective. They may know what the development sector involves and may be familiar with the effects of the changing paradigms. With experience their ways of thinking and vision may have changed. Individuals with less experience in development practice may be gaining knowledge and experience in the process of development practice. They may want to try new ideas and experiment with new approaches, and may have theoretical knowledge if they have specialised training.

Therefore the length of experience in development work was taken as one of the variables of study.

3.10 Review of Literature

The present study aimed at studying the perceptions of development practitioners regarding the selected aspects of development. Related literature was reviewed for the study. While reviewing the literature, it was found that hardly any systematic study was taken up on the development practitioners. Although the working of various voluntary, non–government organisations and government organisations has been studied yet studies focusing on development practitioners and their opinions in development sector are very few. However, some related articles were found in the books, journals and on internet.

3.10.1 Conceptual Review

Development practitioners play a vital role in the development of the nation. They are involved in various stages of development planning, organising, implementing, evaluating and documenting. They should aim at focusing on the complexities underlying development planning and potential pitfalls when attempting to effect social change initiatives.

3.10.1.1. Concept development

Development is a subjective and value loaded concept. At best, development in the context of society could be conceptualised as a set of desirable societal objective which society seeks to achieve. Singh (1999) defined development as "cherished by all individuals, communities and nations, irrespective of their culture, religion and spatial location." Development should therefore, be perceived as a multidimensional process, involving the reorganisation and reorientation of both economic and social systems.

The World Development Report (2003) suggested that new alliances are needed at the local, national and global levels to better address the problems. The burden for development must be shared more widely. Rich countries must further open their markets and cut agricultural subsidies that depress incomes of third world farmers, and they must increase the flow of aid, medicines, and new technologies to developing counties. Governments in the developing world, in turn, must become more accountable and transparent, and ensure that poor people are able to obtain secure land tenure, as well as access to education, health care and other basic services.

Lusk and Mason (1999) observed that sustainable development is an economic strategy which simultaneously pursues increased food and fibre production for the immediate need of the world's poor and the preservation of the common natural resources which will support their children and subsequent generations (Singharoy, 2001:31).

The World Development Report (1997) emphasized on the need for an effective role of the state for social and economic development, but in a new form it writes that the state is central to economic and social development, not as a direct provider for growth but as a partner, catalyst and a facilitator. The world is changing and with it our ideas about the state's role in economic and social development.

The International Commission for Peace and Food (1994) in their report rightly considers the search for new development paradigms to be among the major priorities of the present time. East European Statism has collapsed but there is no place for unfettered capitalism either. Rather than searching for a victor and the vanquished, the urgent need is to find a successor that combine and synthesizes the enlightened values of both systems. The well-being of all individuals should determine social policy and the market economies should undertake to guarantee the right of every citizen to employment.

In the light of the debate inaugurated by the Stockholm Conference (1972) and resumed by the Rio Earth Summit (1992), it was felt that development, in the full sense of the word, should have a social purpose justified by the ethical postulate of intra-generational solidarity and equity, taking the form of a social contract. While the social disparities between nations and within nations have only increased, everything needs to be done to reduce them. This requires privileged groups to ask the question: 'How much is enough?'. The development of man as a whole and of all men can becomes widespread only through the building of 'a civilisation of being in an equitable sharing of having'.

Barbier (1987) stated that the primary objective of sustainable development is reducing the absolute poverty of the world's poor through providing lasting and secure livelihoods that minimise resources depletion, environmental degradation, cultural disruption and social inability (Sharma and Shukla, 1996 :7).

The World Bank (1987) stated that sustainable development aims for promoting growth, alleviating poverty, and protecting the environment are mutually supportive objectives in the long run but not in the short run.

Emphasis on economic development in poverty–stricken country is understandable. However, it does not mean that unless economic development is fully realised, social development should be neglected. Economic growth means not only creation of wealth but also creating people's capacity to create wealth, and this resides in their health, education, knowledge and skills. It is very difficult to separate the two, and this is probably the reason why some experts hold the view that the arbitrary labelling of a group of activities as social development is a conceptual error.

Goulet (1971) explicated in detail his ideas for real development. This description of development was holistic and included a clean environment, growth with equity, provisions of basic needs such as food, shelter, education and medical care; meaningful employment and relationships and others and a harmonious relationship between culture and change. Goulet, a political economist, saw development as freeing men from nature's servitude, from economic backwardness and oppressive technological institutions, from unjust class structures and political exploiters, from cultural and psychic alienation – in short from all of life's inhuman agencies.

Schramm (1964) outlined that importance of education coupled with mass media would accelerate the development process, and noted that the task of the mass media of information and the "new media" of education is to speed and ease the long, slow social transformation required for economic development, and, in particular, to speed and smooth the task of mobilising human resources behind the National effort.

3.10.1.2. Role of various agencies in development

Development agencies are increasingly being used as a vehicle for development. They are becoming a measure of citizen's participation. They work on different issues like poverty, literacy, health, population, environment and many more. They are increasingly demonstrating their own increased social consciousness and social responsibility.

Shah and Iyenger (1998) stated that "the NGOs are generally in better position to both comprehend people's perspective at the local level and share with people the changing perspective at the global level. In this sense they act locally and think globally" (Joshi, 2001: 169).

Chowdhry (1996) in his article "NGOs need both fire and ice" concluded that the new economic policy of globalisation and privatisation may no doubt help in the overall development, creating better employment opportunities and removal of poverty, yet it may throw several other problems, such as consumerism, degradation of environment, women's employment, weakening of family, erosion of traditional value system, poverty syndrome, growing professionalism, large foreign contribution and neo-political affiliations. The NGOs already engaged in these fields will have to reorient their programmes and policies to meet their new challenges. New NGOs are likely to come into being to work in newer areas and fields in order to face newer problems.

Neenawati and Kulkarni (1998) in an article "Role of NGOs in the changing scenario" commented that globalisation of market economy and facilitating industrial development by relaxing government control has created a climate for fresh reflection on the role of government in different areas of its functions, especially in the field of social welfare and development. There is a desire now to hand over the management of programmes of social services, especially where direct contact with people living marginally is involved to voluntary organisations. By acquiring new responsibilities of managing the existing state-administered services for social welfare and development, the NGOs have to harness their special ability and proficiency in enriching these services. They have to ensure that instead of the existing bureaucratic handling of services, they have to initiate innovation and experimentation in organising the services, which are related to the needs of the people instead of people around services. This means that the needs of the beneficiaries are studies and the services related to their fulfilment.

The Planning Commission (1952) in the first five-year plan stated that a major responsibility for organising activities in different fields of social welfare, like the welfare of women and children, social education, community organisation, etc. falls naturally on private voluntary agencies. These private agencies have for long been working in their own humble way, without adequate state aid for the achievement of their objectives with their own leadership, organisation and resources. Any plan for the social and economic generation of the country should take into account the services rendered by these private agencies, and the state should give them the maximum cooperation in strengthening their efforts.

3.10.1.3. Role of development practitioners in the development process

Development practitioners play a vital role in development process. Earlier development was equated with economic growth manifested in ever rising Gross Domestic Product (GDP) and measured against quantifiable parameters till the seventies. The dominant paradigm ruled the nation through industrialisation. At that time extension educators were important agents to bring a change in the lives of the people. But their role was limited to some activities like implementing the programmes planned by higher authority and supervising it. Their major goal was to improve the quality of life of the people.

The "extension functionaries' role was to help the rural people identify their felt needs and to assist them in meeting the needs with the available resources. They are the ones who diffuse knowledge to rural people and key persons who can bring change in the attitudes and behaviour of learners." Later this concept of development was redefined and empowering people to strengthen their capacities became the main objective of development. People were recognised as the partners of development. With this, human development came into existence where human person is the central subject to development.

The concept of sustainable development or people-centred development marked a shift in development theory and practice. Now it is a participatory process of enrichment which spans social, cultural and political dimensions. The issues of health, education, food security, gender empowerment, environment, equality in distribution of benefits, quality life, poverty and many more have come to the forefront. And in a country like India where the evils of poverty, unemployment, illiteracy, ill health are rampant, the need for development management emerged. It aims at creating responsible, self-reliant and resource based communities capable for developing and implementing activities in a manner consistent with the principles of people empowerment.

Here the development practitioners who are directly connected with the people play a vital role. Earlier they had no role to play because economic growth was the only aim but now for people's development, they have a major role to play. They are the key players in development process directly involved in planning and executing the programmes at the grassroots level. They are the change agents and the link between people and planners and vocal players, voicing critiques of the work of others and promoting their views on good development practice. They are essential in maintaining a healthy and viable society. They are dedicated towards the development of the society. It is important that their work should be scrutinised in a professional way. It is therefore critical to explore the extent to which the values and practices they espouse in the development process.

Today with the changing scenario, they need to have some specific skills and competencies. They are close to the people at the grass root level and people put all their demands, needs and problems in front of them. And its not easy to plan programmes for these people at the grassroots level and convince them to adopt the new ideas and knowledge.

3.10.2 Empirical Review

3.10.2.1. Studies conducted abroad

Ashridge and the Corporate Responsibility Group (CRG) (2007) conducted a study on Executive Development for corporate responsibility professionals in UK. The main aim of the study was on the competencies (skills and knowledge sets) they required to be effective. Indepth interviews and questionnaire surveys were used to collect the data. The sample comprised 43 corporate responsibility practitioners. The findings of the study were:

– Most important competencies were seen as influencing and communication skills – cited as important or very important by over ninety percent of respondents.

– Forty percent of respondents devoted on average more than one day a week to influencing and engaging with senior managers and a similar amount of time influencing and engaging with operational managers.

– Expertise in CR was also cited as important or very important by approximately 80 per cent of respondents.

– Understanding the development of CR and emerging issues which was seen as either important or very important for 89 per cent of respondents.

– Building and maintaining leadership in CR was seen as important or very important by 84 per cent of respondents.

– Sixty-eight per cent of respondents believed that building and maintaining leadership in CR will be very important.

– Seventy three percent of respondents believed that effectively and efficiently managing resource, both people and budgets, is going to be important or very important.

– Understanding and working with finance will be important or very important for 57 per cent of practitioners.

– Understanding and working with human resources will be important or very important for 76 per cent of practitioners.

Pezeshki-Rad and Zamani (2005) studied the information-seeking behaviour of extension managers and specialists in Iran to identify the factors that correlate with their behaviour. The population consisted of 38 public extension managers across the country, and 175 public extension specialists who work for Deputy of Extension and Farming System of Iran's Ministry of Agriculture in Tehran.

A questionnaire was developed to explore information-seeking behaviour of extension managers and specialists. The findings of the study were:

- The main motivation for seeking job-related information by both public extension managers and specialists was interest in developing their own job-related information.
- The top three mostly used information sources by extension managers and specialists were Persian books, Persian scientific magazines, and scientific-technical reports. Concerning communication channels, interpersonal communication with colleagues, in-service training courses and scientific-technical conventions were ranked respectively as the three top communication channels used by respondents.
- There was a negative correlation between managers' years of extension work and their information-seeking behaviour.
- For specialists, a significant positive correlation was found between years of education, level of job satisfaction and information-seeking behaviour.

3.10.2.2. Studies conducted in India

Paul (2005) conducted a study on the Voluntary Organisation's contribution to social development. The main aim was to study the pattern or organisational set-up of the voluntary organisation in terms of their objectives, policies, programmes, membership, financial position, staffing pattern and its impact on the beneficiaries. It also aimed to throw light on the role of voluntary organisations in social development in the region of Vadodara district. The sample of the study consisted of 11 policy makers, 22 functionaries and 67 beneficiaries. A structured interview schedule was used for the data collection. The findings of the study are:

- A considerable percentage of the agencies were having health care services (45.5%) and rehabilitative services (45.5%) as their main objective followed by social justice and empowerment (36.4%).

- In majority of agencies both executives and staff members are included in planning process.
- It is rather surprising to note that only less than one-fourth of the agencies had appointed trained social workers.
- Practice of professional and scientific social work is found absent in the voluntary organisation in Vadodara district.
- Only fifty percent beneficiaries were involved in designing various programmes and services.

Iyer (2004) conducted a study on people's perception pertaining to the present temporary shelters and their opinion about the interventions made by governmental, non-governmental and other religious organisations. The sample consisted of 100 beneficiaries of urban areas of Bhuj, Anjar and Bhachau and 20 officials from governmental, non-governmental and other agencies working for rehabilitation of people. The interview schedule was used for the purpose of data collection. The study revealed that 84 per cent of the population received relief material from the government and 16 per cent of the population from NGO. It was observed that nearly fifty percent of population was dependent on government for their relocation and rehabilitation.

Blossom (2000) conducted a study of women social work professionals in different fields. The main aim of the study was to find out whether the knowledge and skills imparted during training are optimally utilised at work place. The sample of the study consisted of 94 women respondents who have completed their postgraduation in social work and working in different fields of social work. A structured interview schedule was used for the data collection. The findings of the study reveal that:

- Social work professionals have a sound base of knowledge of background courses.
- The knowledge of background courses correlates with knowledge of method and field courses irrespective of age and type of organisation and designation.
- Majority of social work professionals use the knowledge of social work methods and processes. The major skill utilised by them is communication skills and values held by them

are confidentiality and humanistic values with some emphasis on responsibility.

Parmar (1999) conducted a study on training as one of the sub-systems of HRD in NGO and assessment of knowledge of the trainers. The sample comprised 60 trainers from different NGOs. A questionnaire was used for the purpose of data collection. The study revealed that training is an instrument to bring change, and develop skills and professional techniques to function better. Majority of the respondents agreed to the statement that training acts as a facilitator of new ideas to trainees and showed a positive attitude towards need based training. Thirty per cent of the respondents had five-six years of work experience followed by nearly twenty five percent of the respondents with three-four years of work experience.

Phillips (1997) conducted a study on functionaries in human care agencies in Indore. The sample consisted of 63 functionaries from government and semi-government agencies working in Indore. An interview schedule was used for data collection. The study signified that the number of respondents who have joined the agency for the main purpose of doing social service are more than double in semi-government organisation as compared to the government organisation. Nearly 50 per cent of the functionaries responded that they get restless during working hours. A majority of the respondents in semi-government organisation felt satisfied with their day's work.

Sen (1995) conducted a research to study the role of voluntary organisations in women development and their services extended. It aimed at the study objectives, finances and personnel of the organisation, and the perceptions of executives, staff and the beneficiaries towards the agency functioning and services in Baroda.

A questionnaire was used to collect the profile of voluntary organisations and separate interview schedule was used for beneficiaries, executives and staff members. Percentages and frequency distribution were used to analyse the data.

Findings revealed that most of the beneficiaries were between 31 and 40 years of age, had low education, were Hindus, married and belonging to low-socio-economic strata of the society. Most of the beneficiaries had joined agency for vocational training of short duration like papad making, masala making, etc., whereas some of the women (24%) joined the organisation for receiving training of stitching, printing. The study reported that most of the women were associated with the agency due to economic needs.

A majority of the women beneficiaries (90%) felt that the agency provided regular and timely services. It was also reported that majority of the women (80%) had a favourable opinion about their organisation. The women found a wide difference in themselves after joining the agency.

The study suggested that beneficiaries should be made aware about the programmes, activities and objectives of their respective voluntary organisations and should be involved in the planning process. NGOs should try to mobilise more on the competencies of staff members. As far as possible NGOs should adopt written communication as a mode of communication to make the programmes more effective.

Kaul (1990) undertook a study to find out the impact of training programme oriented to development of income generating skills, offered by voluntary women's training agencies in Baroda City, on women of low socio-economic status.

Questionnaires were used for administrators, instructors, present and past trainees separately. Data from 24 administrators, 34 instructors, 294 present trainees, 144 past trainees were analysed through percentages and chi-square test Variables considered were age, education qualification, and occupation of the family and income of the of trainees.

A positive impact was found on trainees as there was improvement in their educational, economical and social status.

The Study concluded that government bodies, private agencies like philanthropists could help these agencies by way of financial assistance as it was a bottleneck in their functioning.

The following trends emerged from the empirical review:

— It shows that earlier the emphasis was on development keeping in mind the social and economic aspect.

- Development practitioners being close to the people have a powerful influence on the attitudes and behaviour of the people.
- In most of the studies an interview schedule was used as a tool for data collection.
- Majority of the studies focused on working of different government and non-government organisations and their role was analysed.
- Samples of the referred studies included extension managers, executives and policy makers from agencies, beneficiaries, trainers, etc.
- Studies were conducted during the time span of 10 years, i.e., from 1997-2005.
- Hardly any systematic study was conducted on development practitioners in the present context of development and their role in the development of the nation.

Thus it was felt necessary to undertake the study on perceptions of development practitioners regarding the selected aspects of development.

4

Methodology

The present investigation aimed at studying perceptions of development practitioners regarding the selected aspects of development.

4.1 Population of the Study

Development agencies play an important role in taking up the responsibility of the development of the society. Development practitioners from different development agencies comprised the population of the study.

4.2 Sampling Unit, Technique and Size

Sampling unit refers to the geographical area from where the sample is drawn. The state of Gujarat comprised the sampling unit of the study.

The population of development practitioners is relatively smaller, so it was decided to use the purposive sampling technique for the selection of the sample.

The sample of the study comprised 80 development practitioners from government and non-government organisations and corporate sectors. The development practitioners working in government and non-government organisations and corporate sectors, and those available at the time of data collection were included in the sample. Those practitioners who were on field or out of station were also contacted through mailed questionnaires. Totally 90 questionnaires were received by the researcher. However, 80 of them were included. Ten questionnaires were excluded from the final sample as they were found to be incomplete. Thus the final sample comprised of eighty development practitioners. The population of development practitioners is relatively smaller, so it was decided to use the accidental sampling technique for the selection of the sample. The research method used was survey, as the study involved what and how the development practitioners perceive the selected aspects of development.

4.3 Construction of the Research Tool

A structured questionnaire was prepared to study the perceptions of development practitioners regarding the selected aspects of development. The related content was drawn by referring the sources like books, journals, thesis and articles. Content was also drawn from the experiences of teachers and students of the department involved in field experiences and on development programmes. The researcher also had studied field work-based courses at undergraduate and postgraduate levels, which developed her insight into the role of the development practitioner.

The tool was constructed in English and later translated into Gujarati for the convenience of the development practitioners.

4.3.1 Description of the Tools

A structured questionnaire was prepared. The questionnaire consisted of equal appearing interval scale. As the research study aimed at studying the perceptions of the development practitioners on selected aspects of development and how and to what extent the development practitioners hold the perceptions of development, it was decided to prepare a questionnaire consisting of equally appearing interval scale and checklist. The questionnaire consisted of the following seven sections:

Section I: It consisted of the profile of development practitioners such as their age, sex, educational qualification, marital status, type of organisation in which they were working, their designation, experience of work, activities in which they are involved, target group they catered to, focus areas of their development programmes and sources of funds for their projects.

Section II: This included the items on various perceptions attached to the meaning of development work such as removal of poverty, enlarging people's choices, building up an enabling environment for people to enjoy a long, healthy and creative life, establishment of law and order. All the items were positive in nature as the meaning of development reflected some kind of progress or betterment in the existing condition. A three-point scale was prepared for this purpose.

Section III: It consisted of the priority areas of concern for development such as literacy, health, poverty alleviation, child labour, women's rights, gender empowerment, water and sanitation, and so on. Different areas were listed and a checklist was prepared.

Section IV: This section included the competencies required by development practitioners such as communication skills, persuasive skills, futuristic vision, managerial skills, leadership skills, problem-solving ability, ability to mobilise resources for development programmes, documentation skills, commitment for the cause and many more. All the statements were positive in nature and a three-point scale was used for this purpose.

Section V: This section dealt with the approaches of development as a basis for planning development programmes such as participatory approach, top-down, localised, multidimensional, development support communication, linear, diffusion of innovation and mass media, and modernisation approach. A three-point scale was prepared for this section.

Section VI: It included the problems which development practitioners come across at various stages of development work such as financial, social, staff related, resources related and other miscellaneous problems. A three-point scale was used for this purpose.

SectionVII: This section consisted of the items on the challenges development practitioners face such as collecting funds for development programmes, working with downtrodden groups, working in harsh conditions, encouraging people to participate. A three-point scale was used.

Further three open-ended questions were prepared on the communication strategies used in development programmes, the indicators used to measure development work and practitioner's motivation to join development sector.

Table 1. Description of Research Tool

Section	*Content*	*Tool*	*Response System*
I.	Profile of the development practitioners	Checklist	-
II.	Meanings attached to development	Interval scale	3-point response system
III.	Priority areas for development	Checklist	-
IV.	Competencies required by development practitioners	Interval scale	3-point response system
V.	Approaches for planning development programme	Interval scale	3-point response system
VI.	Problems development practitioners face such financial, social, staff & resources related and other miscellaneous	Interval scale	3-point response system
VII.	Challenges development practitioners face	Interval scale	3-point response system

The questionnaire was given to three experts in the field of development practice for checking the content, clarity and completeness of language and suitability of the response system. The experts were from the Department of Extension Communication, the Faculty of Family and Community Sciences, Vadodara and Non-Government Organisation's personnel working in the field of rural development and Environment Education. The suggestions given by the experts were incorporated in the tool.

The research tool constructed in English was later translated in Gujarati and it was checked by the expert in Gujarati language.

Pretesting of the tool was done with five development practitioners. Two English questionnaires and three Guajarati questionnaires were used for the pretesting. The purpose of pretesting was to know the difficulty in following the questionnaire and to check the clarity of the language. The tool was clear and understandable and the development practitioners took around forty five minutes to fill up one questionnaire.

4.4 Collection of the Data

The data were collected in the month of November-December 2007 and January 2008. The data were collected from the development practitioners through personal contact and mailed questionnaires.

The investigator personally collected the data by contacting the development practitioners of Gujarat at an International Conference on Education for Sustainable Development held at the Centre for Environment Education (CEE), Ahmedabad. The organisations from which data were collected were as followed:

Government organisations

1. Water and Sanitation Management Organisation (WASMO), Surendranagar, Gandhinagar.
2. District Rural Development Agency (DRDA), Vadodara.
3. Zilla Panchayat, Vadodara.

Non-Government organisations

1. Center for Environment Education (CEE), Ahmedabad.
2. Pravah, Ahmedabad.
3. Viksat, Ahmedabad.
4. Baroda Citizens Council, Vadodara.
5. Olakh, Vadodara.
6. Shroffs Foundation, Vadodara.
7. Shishu Milap, Vadodara.

Corporate sectors

1. Asian Brown Boveri (ABB), Vadodara.

2. Deepak Foundation, Vadodara.
3. Larsen and Toubro (L&T) Vadodara.

4.5 Scoring and Categorisation of Data

4.5.1 Scoring and Categorisation of Variables of Study

Variables selected for the study were categorised as follows:

Table 2. Categorisation of Variables

Sr. No.	*Variables*	*Basis*	*Category*
1	Age	Below mean	Younger
		Mean and above mean	Older
2	Sex	-	Male
		-	Female
3	Educational qualifications	Secondary Higher Secondary Diploma/PTC Graduation P.G. Diploma	Average
		M. Phil. Postgraduation Doctorate	High
4	Type of development organisation	-	Government
		-	Non-Government
		-	Corporate
5	Length of experience	Less than 5years to 5 years	Less
		Above 5 years up to 10 years	Moderate
		Above 10 years	More

4.5.2 Scoring and Categorisation of Other Characteristics of Development Practitioners

Table 3. Categorisation of Other Characteristics

Sr. No.	*Others Characteristics*	*Basis*	*Category*
1.	Marital status		Married

(Contd...)

(Contd...)

		-	Unmarried
2.	Designation	Manager Head Executives Coordinators	Executive
		Associates Project engineers Consultant Counselor	Project coordinator & consultant
		Trainer ORW Field worker Community entrepreneur JAO	Field workers
3.	Specialised training for development practitioner	Social work Rural management Development Communication	Trained
		Arts Commerce Science	Not trained
2.	Family member's involvement in	-	Involved
	development work	-	Not involved

4.5.3 Scoring and Categorisation of the Aspects of the Study

The aspects in which the perceptions of the development practitioners were studied were the meanings attached to development, approaches to development, competencies required by development practitioners, problems and challenges for development. A three-point scale was used to study the extent of the perceptions.

Item-wise Intensity Indices (I.I.) and percentages were calculated to study the meanings of development, competencies required by development practitioners, approaches to development and problems and challenges development practitioners face. The range for item-wise intensity indices for the perceptions of the development practitioners regarding the above listed aspects was decided as follows:

Range	*Extent of Perceptions*
2.60 – 3.00	Perceived to great extent
1.60 – 2.59	Perceived to some extent
1.00 – 1.59	Perceived to less extent

Table 4. Aspect wise Maximum and Minimum Possible Scores

Section	*Aspects Of Study*	*No. Of Items*	*Maximum Scores*	*Minimum Scores*
II	Meanings of development	30	90	30
IV	Competencies required by development practitioners	32	96	32
V	Approaches for Planning development programmes	8	24	8
VI	Problems development practitioners face.	37	111	37
VII	Challenges development practitioners face.	10	30	10

Scoring for the priority areas of concern for development was done as follows:

Range	*Description*
70 percent and above	Priority area of high concern
50 percent to 69 percent	Priority area of moderate concern
49 percent and below	Priority area of less concern

4.6 Plan of Statistical Analysis of Data

Table 5. Different Statistical measures used for the analysis of the data

Sr. No.	*Purpose*	*Statistical Measures*
1.	Profile of the development practitioners.	Percentages
2.	Item-wise perceptions of development practitioners regarding the meanings attached to development.	Percentages & intensity indices

(Contd...)

(Contd...)

3.	Item-wise perceptions of development practitioners regarding the priority areas of concern for development.	Percentages
4.	Item-wise perceptions of development practitioners regarding the competencies required by development practitioners.	Percentages and intensity indices
5.	Item-wise perceptions of development practitioners regarding the approaches used as a basis for planning development programmes.	Percentages and intensity indices
6.	Item-wise perceptions of development practitioners regarding the problems that they face in doing development work.	Percentages and intensity indices
7.	Item-wise perceptions of development practitioners regarding the challenges faced by development practitioners in doing development work.	Percentages and intensity indices
8.	Overall differences in the perceptions of development practitioners regarding their problems in relation to the selected variables.	F – Test (ANOVA) t – test

For 't' test the formula used was:

$$t = \frac{X1 - X2}{\frac{SP^2}{n_1} + \frac{SP^2}{n_2}}$$

$$SP^2 = \frac{(n_1 - 1)\, S_1^2 + (n_2 - 1)\, S_2^2}{n_1 + n_2 - 2}$$

Where, X_1 = mean of $group_1$

X_2 = mean of $group_2$

n_1 = number of $group_1$

n_2 = number of $group_2$

df = $n_1 + n_2 - 2$

S_1 = S.D. of $group_1$

S_2 = S.D. of $group_2$

Sp^2 = pooled variance

Formula for ANOVA (F - test) used was:

$$F = \frac{\text{Large variance}}{\text{Small variance}}$$

$$\text{Or} = \frac{\text{Between group variance}}{\text{Within group variance}}$$

Between Group Variance = Variance in the mean of each groups from the total mean of all variance groups

Within Group Variance = Average variability of scores within groups.

5

Findings

The present investigation aimed at studying the perceptions of the development practitioners regarding the selected aspects of development.

5.1 Profile of Development Practitioners

Table 1. Variable-wise Percentage Distribution of Development Practitioners

N = 80

Sr. No.	*Variables*	*Percentage*
1.	Age group:	
	Younger	62.50
	Older	37.50
2.	Sex:	
	Male	55.00
	Female	45.00
3.	Educational Qualifications:	
	Average level	32.50
	High level	67.50
4.	Type of Development Organisation:	
	Government	26.25
	Non-Government	50.00
	Corporate	23.75
5.	Length of experience in development work:	
	Less	48.75
	Moderate	30.00
	More	21.25

Table 6 reveals that age-wise, a majority of the development practitioners were younger (62.50 percent) while little less than 40 percent of the development practitioners were older. Sex-wise, a little more than 50 percent of the development practitioners were males, whereas, little less than 50 percent of the development practitioners were females.

The table also reveals that majority of the development practitioners had high level of educational qualification (67.50 percent), whereas, little more than 30 percent of the development practitioners had an average level of educational qualification. With regard to the type of development organisation, 50 percent of the development practitioners belonged to non–government organisations, whereas, little less than 30 percent of the development practitioners belonged to government organisations followed by little less than one-fourth of the development practitioners belonging to the corporate sector.

N = 80

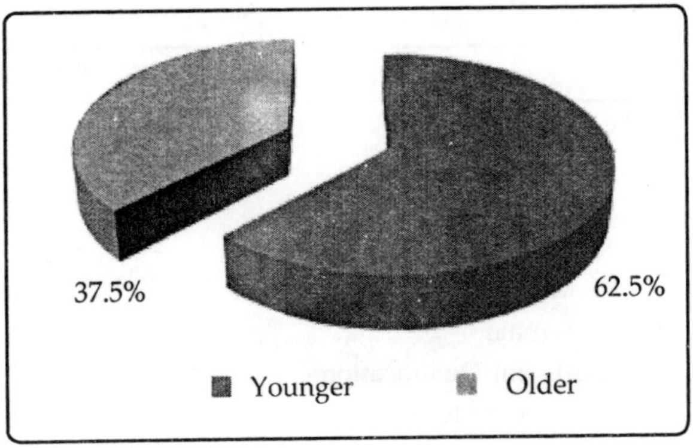

Figure 1: Age of the Development Practitioners

The table also shows that nearly 50 percent of the development practitioners were less experienced in development work, whereas, 30 percent of the development practitioners were moderately experienced in development work followed by little less than one-fourth of the development practitioners having more experience in development work.

N = 80

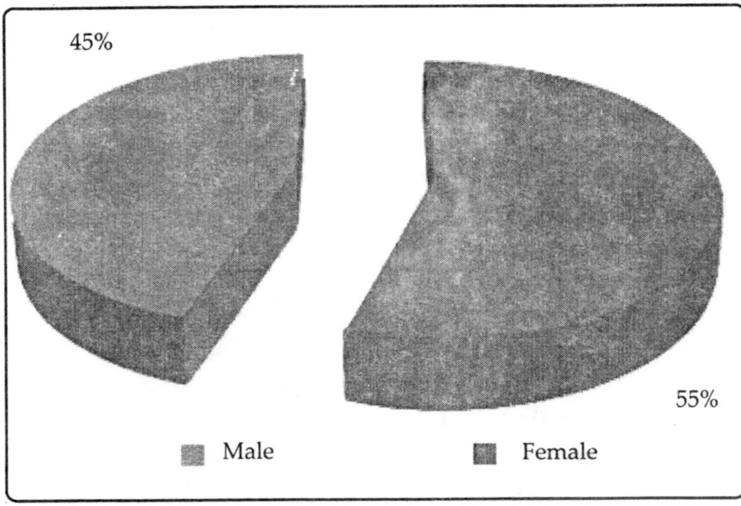

Figure 2: Sex-wise Development Practitioners

Table 7. Percentage Distribution of Development Practitioners According to Other Characteristics

N = 80

Sr. No.	*Other Characteristics*	*Percentage*
1.	Marital status	
	Married	72.80
	Unmarried	27.50
2.	Present Designation:	
	Executive	25.00
	Project coordinator and consultant	40.00
	Field worker	35.00
3.	Specialised training for working as development practitioner:	
	Trained	65.00
	Not trained	35.00
4.	Family members involvement in development work:	
	Involved	25.00
	Not involved	75.00

Table 7 reveals that according to marital status high majority of the development practitioners were married, whereas, one-fourth of them were unmarried. With regard to the present designation, 40 percent of the development practitioners were project coordinators and consultants, whereas, a little more than 30 percent of the development practitioners were field workers followed by 25 percent of the development practitioners being executives in the development organisations.

N=80

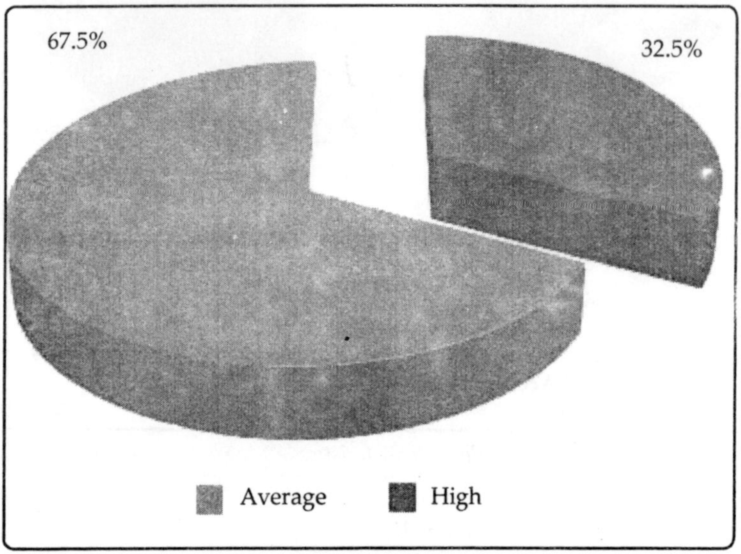

Figure 3: Educational Qualifications of the Development Practitioners

As far as specialised training in development work was concerned, a majority of the development practitioners were specially trained for working as the development practitioners. They were trained in the areas like rural development, social work, rural studies, disaster management, clinical and community psychology, target intervention training, development communication, integrated rural personnel management, whereas, a little more than 30 percent of the development practitioners did not undergo specialised training.

The table also shows that family members of high majority of the development practitioners were not involved in development work, whereas, family members of one-fourth of the development practitioners were involved in the development work as social worker, anganwadi worker, school teacher, extension worker, etc.

N = *80*

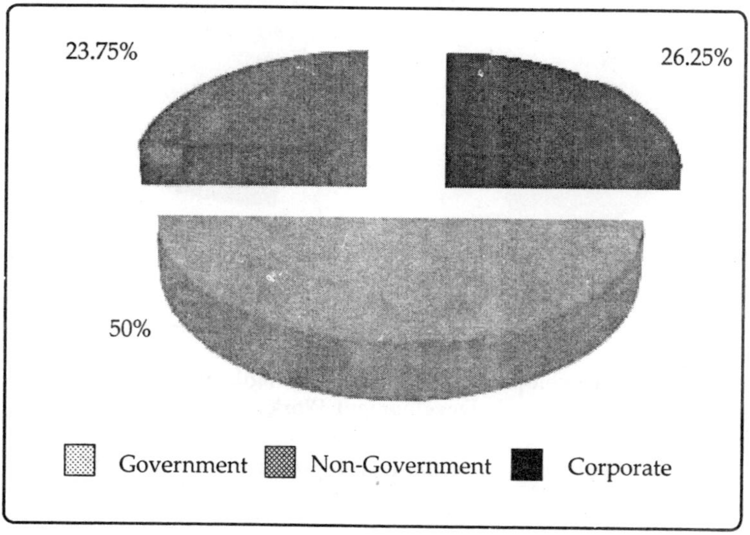

Figure 4: Type of Development Organisation of the Development Practitioners

Table 8 reveals that health was a major focus area of development programmes for majority of the development practitioners, whereas, little more than 50 percent of the development practitioners focused on water and sanitation in their development programmes.

Nearly 50 percent of the development practitioners focused on income generation in their development programmes followed by a little more than 40 percent of the development practitioners focusing on literacy in their development programmes.

N = 80

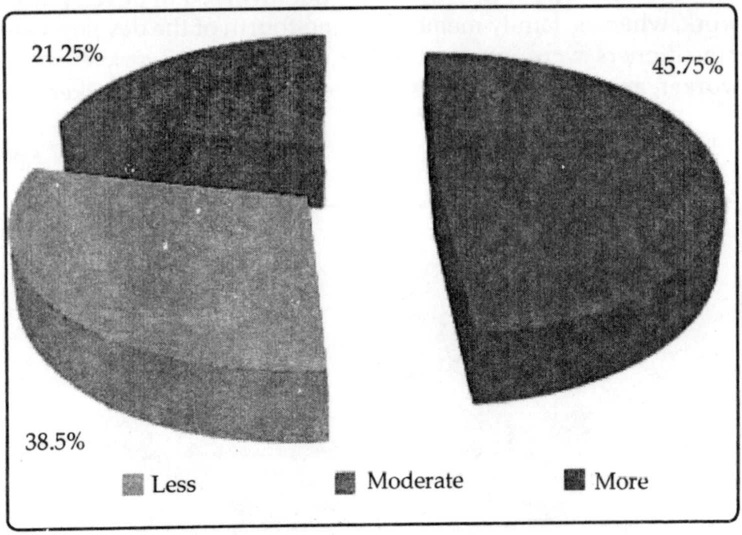

Figure 5: Development Practitioner's Length of Experience in Development Work

Table 8. Focus Areas of the Development Practitioners' Work

N = 80

Sr. No.	*Focus area*	*Percentage*
1.	Health	60.00
2.	Water and sanitation	56.25
3.	Income generation	47.50
4.	Literacy	42.50
5.	Environment	36.25
6.	Poverty alleviation	35.00
7.	Reproductive health	32.50
8.	Human rights	28.75
9.	Infrastructure development	27.50
10.	Any other (livelihoods, mental health, rehabilitation of street children, wage employment, animal husbandry, self-help groups, etc.)	13.75

N = *80*

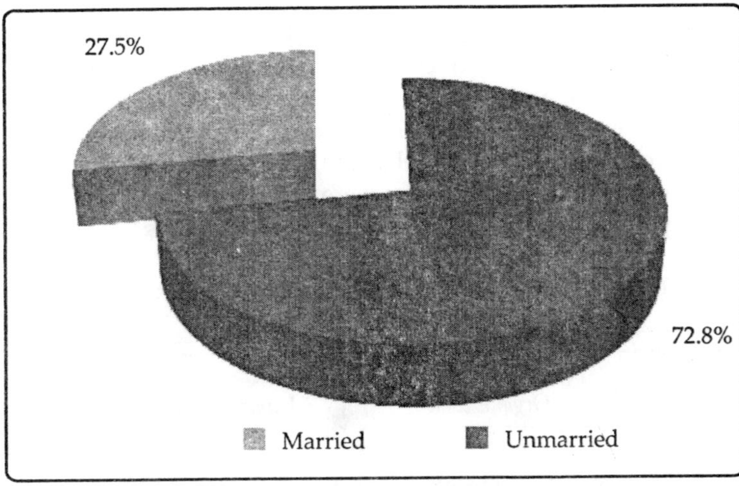

Figure 6: Marital Status of the Development Practitioners

N = *80*

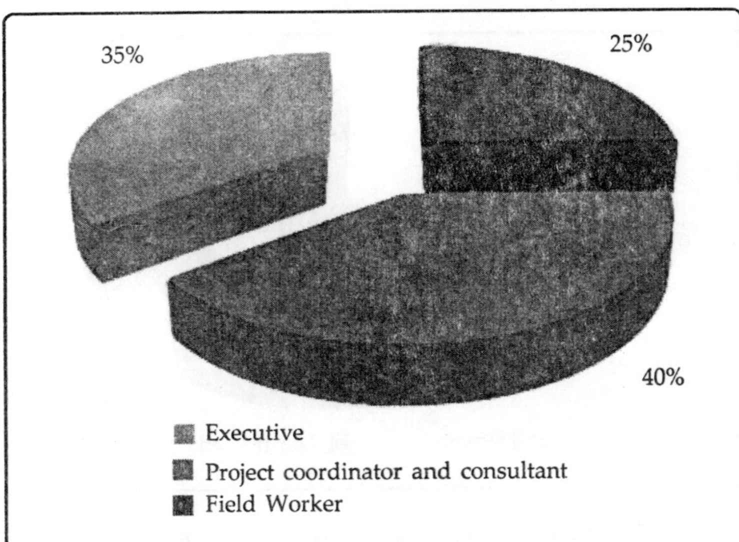

Figure 7: Designation of the Development Practitioners in the Organisation

A little more than one-third of the development practitioners focused on environment, poverty alleviation and reproductive health for the development programmes followed by little more than one-fourth of the development practitioners focusing on human rights and infrastructure development for their development programmes. The areas like livelihoods, mental health, rehabilitation of street children, wage employment, animal husbandry and self-help groups were perceived as priority areas by only 10 percent of the development practitioners.

Table 9. Staff Strength in Development Organisations

N = 80

Sr. No.	*Type of Development Organisation*	*Number Of Staff Members*
1.	Government organisations	5 – 100
2.	Non government organisations	15 – 125
3.	Corporate sectors	4 - 40

N = 80

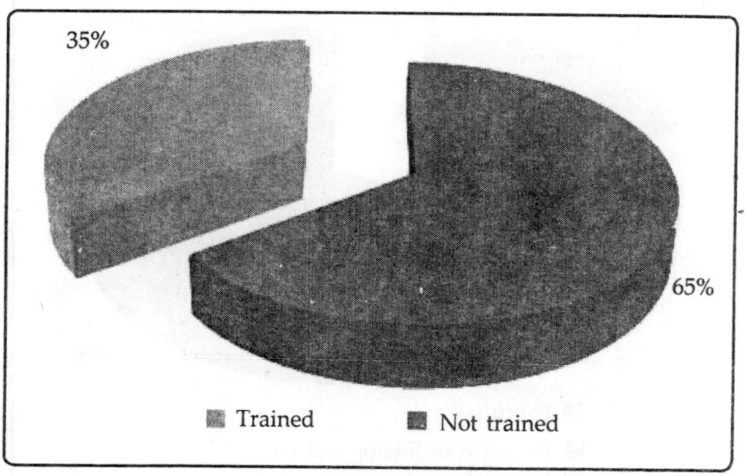

Figure 8: Training of Working as Development Practitioner

Table 9 reveals that the number of staff members working in development-related departments in government organisations ranged from 5 to 100 members, whereas, the number of staff members in non -government organisations ranged from 15 to 125 members working in development related departments followed by 4 – 40 members in the corporate sector.

Table 10. Target Groups being catered by Development Practitioners

N = 80

Sr. No.	*Target Group*	*Percentage*
1.	Women	83.75
2.	Children	72.50
3.	Youth	71.25
4.	Men	55.00
5.	Elderly	45.00
6.	Differently Abled	30.00

N = 80

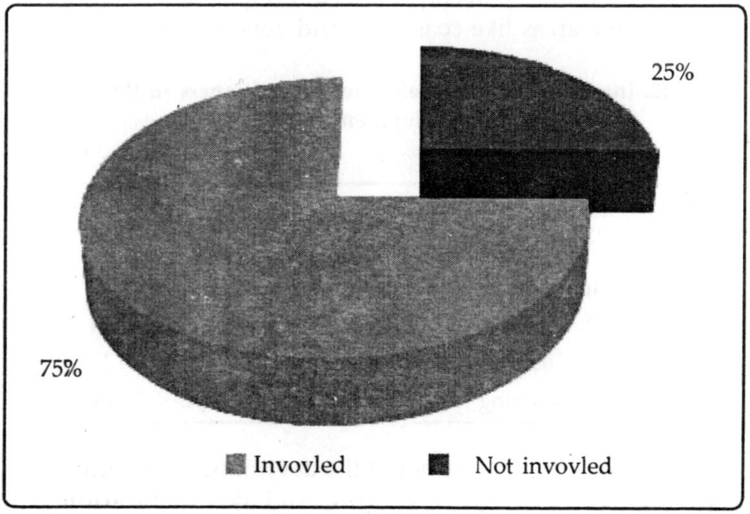

Figure 9: Involvement of Development Practitioner's Family Members in Development Work

Table 10 reveals that a high majority of the development practitioners had women as their target group followed by a majority of the development practitioners catering to children or youth as their target groups. Little more than 50 percent of the development practitioners catered to men's groups, whereas, a little less than 50 percent of the development practitioners catered to the elderly as their target group.

Table 11. Geographical Areas of Development Practitioners' Work

N = 80

Sr. No.	*Geographical Area of Work*	*Percentage*
1.	Rural	70.00
2.	Tribal	36.25
3.	Urban	33.75
4.	Hilly	10.00
5.	Others (coastal, arid zone, forest, etc.)	03.75

Table 11 shows that 70 percent of the development practitioners worked in the rural areas followed by more than one-third of the development practitioners working in tribal or urban areas, whereas, only four percent of the development practitioners worked in the areas like coastal or arid zone or forest area.

Table 12. Involvement of Development Practitioners in the Stages of Development Work

N = 80

Sr. No.	*Stages of Development Work*	*Percentage*
1.	Report writing and documentation	70.00
2.	Implementing	67.50
3.	Planning	66.25
4.	Evaluating	66.25
5.	Supervising	56.25

Table 12 reveals that 70 percent of the development practitioners were involved in report writing and documentation of development work in their organisation, whereas, a majority of the development practitioners were involved in implementing, planning and evaluating development activities. A little more than 50 percent of the development practitioners were involved in only supervising the development work in the organisation.

Table 13. Sources of Funds for Development Projects

N = 80

Sr. No.	*Sources of Funds*	*Percentage*
1.	State government	58.75
2.	Central government	45.00
3.	International funding agency	33.75
4.	Individual donations to the Organisation	33.75
5.	Trust	26.25
6.	Corporate	18.75

Table 13 shows that nearly 60 percent of the development practitioners reported that the state government provided funds for their projects followed by 45 percent of them reporting that central government provided funds, whereas, equal percentage of the development practitioners reported that international funding agency and individual donations were the source of funds for their projects.

5.1.1 Meanings Attached to Development

Table 14

Percentages and Item-Wise Intensity Indices Showing Perceptions of Development Practitioners Regarding Meanings Attached to Development

N = 80

Sr. No.	*Meanings attached to development*	*GE (%)*	*SE (%)*	*LE (%)*	*I.I.*
1.	Building up an enabling environment for people to enjoy a long, healthy and creative life.	78.75	13.75	7.50	2.71

(Contd...)

(Contd...)

2.	Fulfilling basic needs of people.	77.50	13.75	8.75	2.69
3.	Improving people's lifestyles through better education.	76.25	15.00	8.75	2.68
4.	Developing positive attitudes and values of life amongst people.	72.50	20.00	7.50	2.65
5.	Development and improvement of institutions like schools, colleges, etc.	73.75	15.00	11.25	2.63
6.	Providing opportunity to every human being to grow and reach their full potentials.	67.50	27.50	5.00	2.63
7.	Preparing and organising people for development.	70.00	20.00	10.00	2.60
8.	Economic growth / increase in per capita income.	65.00	25.00	10.00	2.55
9.	Change in popular attitudes (such as attitudes towards gender, poor people, minorities, etc.).	58.75	32.50	8.75	2.50
10.	Improving human relations in society.	55.00	38.75	6.25	2.49
11.	Sustained growth of individuals to cope with the continuous changes.	55.00	38.75	6.25	2.49
12.	Removal of poverty.	65.00	17.50	17.50	2.48
13.	People being able to live a satisfying life.	62.50	22.50	15.00	2.48
14.	Participatory process of social change.	56.25	31.25	12.50	2.44
15.	Conserving the environment for future generation.	58.75	25.00	16.25	2.42
16.	Improving people's lifestyle through improved individual income.	53.75	31.25	15.00	2.39

(Contd...)

(Contd...)

17.	Establishment of law and order in society.	51.25	35.00	13.75	2.38
18.	Decent living and security for people within their homes.	52.50	30.00	17.50	2.35
19.	Lessening of disparity between regions, classes. (Caste, religion, etc.)	51.25	32.50	16.25	2.35
20.	Provision of telecommunications and information technology for better communication, information and education.	51.25	32.50	16.25	2.35
21.	Vulnerability reduction and ability enhancement of stakeholders regarding adoptability and mitigation.	51.25	31.25	17.50	2.34
22.	Building up of technological infrastructure for speeding the process of development.	52.50	27.50	20.00	2.33
23.	Enlarging people's choices.	40.00	47.50	12.50	2.28
24.	Equal distribution of income and wealth.	42.50	37.50	20.00	2.23
25.	Political freedom to people of all sections.	41.25	37.50	21.25	2.20
26.	Modernisation of society through shedding superstitions.	42.50	32.50	25.00	2.17
27.	Changing the society from traditional to modern (in relations, thinking, methods of production, living styles, etc.).	30.00	51.25	18.75	2.11
28.	People's familiarity with mechanical gadgets.	28.75	41.25	30.00	1.99
29.	Modernisation of society through shedding tribalism.	30.00	35.00	35.00	1.93
30.	Modernisation of society through shedding feudalism.	18.75	45.00	36.25	1.85

Table 14 reveals that the item-wise intensity indices for the perceptions of the development practitioners regarding the meanings attached to development ranged from 2.71 to 1.85.

The development practitioners perceived development as building up an enabling environment for people to enjoy a long, healthy and creative life, fulfilling basic needs of the people, improving positive attitudes and values amongst people, providing opportunity to every individual to grow and reach their full potentials, developing and improving educational institutions, and preparing and organising people for development to a great extent. On the other hand, the meanings like development meant economic growth, conservation of environment, modernisation of society, sustained growth of individuals to cope with continuous changes and political freedom were perceived by the development practitioners to some extent.

It is also evident from the table that percentage-wise a high majority of the development practitioners perceived the following meanings of development to a great extent:

- Enabling environment for enjoying long, healthy life.
- Fulfilling basic needs.
- Providing opportunity to every individual to grow and reach their full potentials.
- Preparing and organising people for development.
- Developing and improving educational institutions.

5.1.2 Priority Areas of Concern for Development

Table 15 reveals that a high majority of the development practitioners perceived literacy, health education, poverty alleviation and gender empowerment and water and sanitation as priority areas of high concern for development followed by a majority of the development practitioners perceiving environment education, women's rights, population education, income generation and natural resources management as priority areas of moderate concern for development.

The table also shows that a little more than 40 percent of the development practitioners perceived the areas like rural housing development, waste management, vocational skill development, technological development, entrepreneurship development and value / cultural education, as priority areas of less concern for development.

Table 15

Percentage Showing Perceptions of Development Practitioners Regarding Priority Areas of Concern for Development

N = 80

Sr. No.	*Priority Areas*	*Percentage*
1.	Literacy	91.25
2.	Health education	81.25
3.	Poverty alleviation	72.50
4.	Gender empowerment	71.25
5.	Water and sanitation	70.00
6.	Environment education	68.75
7.	Women's rights	63.75
8.	Population education	62.50
9.	Income generation	62.50
10.	Natural resource management	61.25
11.	Child labour	53.75
12.	Sustainable agriculture development	51.25
13.	Sex education	46.25
14.	Reproductive health education	46.25
15.	Rural housing development	43.75
16.	Waste management	43.75
17.	Vocational skill development	42.50
18.	Technological development	42.50
19.	Entrepreneurship development	42.50
20.	Value / cultural education	41.25
21.	Personality development	33.75
22.	Social forestry	32.50
23.	Spiritual development	31.25
24.	Political empowerment	30.00

5.1.3 Competencies Required by Development Practitioners

Table 16

Percentages and Item-Wise Intensity Indices Showing Perceptions of Development Practitioners Regarding Competencies Required in Their Work

N = 80

Sr. No.	*Competencies*	*GE (%)*	*SE (%)*	*LE (%)*	*I.I.*
1.	Communication skills	91.25	6.25	2.50	2.89
2.	Ability to lead the group	90.00	8.75	1.25	2.89
3.	Ability to work with the team	87.50	11.25	1.25	2.86
4.	Problem-solving ability	86.25	10.00	3.75	2.83
5.	Confidence in carrying out development work	81.25	16.25	2.50	2.79
6.	Ability to judge the situation for immediate action	78.75	21.25	-	2.79
7.	Ability to analyse the situation	76.25	23.75	-	2.76
8.	Organisational and planning skills	80.00	15.00	5.00	2.75
9.	Tactful handling of critical situations in development work	77.50	18.75	3.75	2.74
10.	Commitment for the cause, dedication to the work and sensitivity to stakeholders.	76.25	21.25	2.50	2.74
11.	Futuristic vision for development	76.25	20.00	3.75	2.73
12.	Ability to take initiative for development work	76.25	18.75	5.00	2.71
13.	Ability to create work culture where each member in team can find his/her own niche and give their best.	73.25	22.50	3.75	2.70
14.	Ability to evaluate development programme	71.25	23.75	5.00	2.66
15.	Managerial skills	70.00	26.25	3.75	2.66
16.	Skill to create learning environment.	65.00	35.00	–	2.65

(Contd...)

(Contd...)

17.	Ability to mobilise resources for development programme.	67.50	28.75	3.75	2.64
18.	Flexibility to adjust to changes required in development.	66.25	30.00	3.75	2.63
19.	Ability to resolve conflicts	65.00	32.50	2.50	2.63
20.	Documentation skills	67.50	26.25	6.25	2.61
21.	Ability of networking at various levels.	65.00	31.25	3.75	2.61
22.	Alertness in identifying the needs and problems of community	65.00	31.25	3.75	2.61
23.	Ability to cope with stress / pressure in development programme	68.75	22.50	8.75	2.60
24.	Ability to generate human resources in development programme	67.50	25.00	7.50	2.60
25.	Persuasive skills	63.75	32.50	3.75	2.60
26.	Managing development practice related information.	61.25	32.50	6.25	2.55
27.	Indepth knowledge and expertise of subject matter.	73.75	6.25	20.00	2.54
28.	Ability to monitor development programme	58.75	36.25	5.00	2.54
29.	Ability to judge and keep right balance of physical targets and desirable developmental process.	56.25	35.00	8.75	2.48
30.	Ability to utilise non-human resources in development programme.	52.50	37.50	10.00	2.42
31.	Indepth knowledge and expertise of development process.	65.00	7.50	27.50	2.38
32.	Indepth knowledge and expertise of human psychology / relations.	60.00	8.75	31.25	2.29

Table 16 reveals that the item-wise intensity indices for the perceptions of the development practitioners regarding the competencies required by the development practitioners ranged from 2.89 to 2.29.

The highest intensity indices were found for competencies like communication skills and ability to lead the group and work with the team. This means that these competencies were perceived to a great extent by the development practitioners. The competencies like managing development related information, indepth knowledge and expertise of development process, subject matter and human relations, ability to judge, monitor and utilise non human resources in development programmes were perceived to some extent by the development practitioners.

Percentage wise high majority of the development practitioners perceived the following competencies to be required to a great extent:

- Communication skills
- Ability the lead and work with the team
- Problem solving ability
- Ability to judge the situation
- Organisational and planning skills
- Commitment and futuristic vision

5.1.4 Approaches to be used as a basis for Planning Development Programmes

Table 17

Percentages and Item Wise Intensity Indices Showing Perceptions of Development Practitioners Regarding Approaches to be used as Basis for Planning Development Programmes

N = 80

Sr. No.	*Approaches*	*GE (%)*	*SE (%)*	*LE (%)*	*I.I.*
1.	Participatory approach focusing on involvement of target group in all stages of the development process.	83.75	13.75	2.20	2.81

(Contd...)

2.	Development support communication approach which stresses on grassroots level development & participating in using small media as support in communication.	77.50	18.75	3.75	2.74
3.	Localised approach which stressing on use of local resources to fulfil local needs.	77.50	16.25	6.25	2.71
4.	Multidimensional approach focusing on multiple concept for development rather than focusing on one single issue.	65.00	30.00	5.00	2.59
5.	Diffusion of innovation focusing on assessing the needs of target group helping people to fulfil their needs by adoption of innovations.	61.25	36.25	2.50	2.58
6.	Mass media and modernisation approach stressing on use of mass media in adopting the innovations.	48.75	46.25	5.00	2.44
7.	Top-down approach focusing on the programmes and policies planned by higher authorities in government, etc.	30.00	35.00	35.00	1.95
8.	Linear approach stressing on only one aspect at time.	23.75	47.50	28.75	1.95

5.1.5 Problems Development Practitioners face

Table 17 reveals that the item wise intensity indices for the perceptions of the development practitioners regarding the approaches to be used as a basis for planning development programmes ranged from 2.81 to 1.95.

Table 18

Percentages and Item-Wise Intensity Indices Showing Perceptions Regarding Problems that Development Practitioners face in doing Development Work

N = 80

Sr. No.	*Problems*	*GE (%)*	*SE (%)*	*LE (%)*	*I.I.*
1.	*Financial problems*				
	a. Getting funds from government or funding agency is time consuming.	45.00	38.75	16.25	2.29
	b. There is a lack of funds for development programmes.	47.50	30.00	22.50	2.25
	c. There is lack of freedom in utilising funds.	38.75	35.00	26.25	2.13
	Social problems				
	a. There exists poverty in the society.	58.75	35.00	6.25	2.53
	b. There is illiteracy in the society.	56.25	38.75	5.00	2.51
	c. People have indifferent attitude towards development work.	53.72	28.75	17.50	2.36
	d. There is too much of caste consciousness in society.	45.00	38.75	16.25	2.29
	e. Superstitions still exist in the society.	42.50	43.75	13.75	2.29
	f. There is existence of gender inequality in the society.	40.00	45.00	15.00	2.25
	g. There is too much of class consciousness in society.	38.75	38.75	22.50	2.16
2.	*Staff-related problems*				
	a. There is lack of job security for development practitioner.	53.75	32.50	13.75	2.40

(Contd...).

(Contd...)

b.	The salary for development practitioner.	43.75	37.50	18.75	2.25
c.	No freedom or autonomy to take decision.	36.25	27.50	36.25	2.21
d.	Development practitioners lack in motivation to continue in development sector.	40.00	40.00	20.00	2.20
e.	There is lack of other privileges and benefits for development practitioner.	36.25	40.00	23.75	2.13
f.	Inadequate number of staff members to carry out targeted projects.	32.50	45.00	22.50	2.10
g.	Staff members have casual approach in doing development work.	30.00	45.00	25.00	2.05
h.	There is lack of trained professionals for development work.	38.75	43.75	17.50	2.05
i.	There is lack of commitment among development practitioner in doing development work.	30.00	41.25	28.25	2.01
j.	There is lack of interest among development practitioner in doing development work.	26.25	46.25	27.50	1.99
k.	There are no modern management systems in work place.	28.75	40.00	31.25	1.98
l.	Intellectual vacuum over a period of time in the organisation.	28.75	38.75	32.50	1.96
m.	Lack of readiness to travel for field work.	26.25	36.25	37.50	1.89
n.	Working hours are inconvenient for staff members.	25.00	38.75	36.25	1.89

(Contd...)

(Contd...)

3. *Resources-related problems*				
a. Deadlines of project restrict sufficient time allotment for each development programme.	38.75	35.00	26.25	2.13
b. There is lack of transportation for shifting beneficiaries to participate in development programme.	21.25	47.50	31.25	1.90
c. There is lack of transportation for staff member to go to development site.	25.00	35.00	40.00	1.85
d. There are inadequate number of equipments for development programme such as TV, white boards, OHP, and other materials.	20.00	41.25	38.75	1.81
e. There is improper infrastructure for development work such as rooms, fans, water facility, tube-lights, etc.	16.25	46.25	37.50	1.79
4. *Other problems*				
a. People are not aware about development programme.	47.50	38.75	13.75	2.34
b. Local leaders dominate in development work.	47.50	37.50	15.00	2.33
c. The correct (exact) amounts of allotted funds don't reach the beneficiaries for development programme	50.00	31.25	18.75	2.31

(Contd...)

(Contd...)

d. More time is spent in administration/finance than programmatic.	40.00	48.75	11.25	2.29
e. Political interference in development work.	37.50	48.75	13.75	2.24
f. People do not participate in development programme.	40.00	41.25	18.75	2.21
g. Staff members are not committed to their duties in development sector.	32.50	32.50	35.00	1.98
h. No opportunity for lateral learning and sharing.	26.25	43.75	30.00	1.96

Participatory, development support communication and localised approaches were perceived as a basis for planning development programmes to a great extent by the development practitioners whereas, multidimensional, diffusion of innovation, mass media and modernisation, top-down and linear approaches were perceived as a basis for planning development programmes to some extent. Percentage-wise also the similar trends emerged.

Table 18 reveals that the item-wise intensity indices for the perceptions of the development practitioners regarding the problems they come across in doing development work ranged from 2.53 to 1.79.

Extent-wise majority of the development practitioners perceived the social problems like existence of poverty and illiteracy in the society, people's indifferent attitude towards development work and staff related problems like lack of job security for development practitioners to a great extent.

It further reveals that nearly 50 percent of the development practitioners perceived financial problems like lack of funds for development programmes and time consuming activity for getting funds from government or funding agencies to a great extent.

As far as the social problems were concerned nearly 40 percent of the development practitioners perceived the following problems to a great extent:

- Too much of caste and class consciousness in the society
- Existence of superstitions and gender inequality in the society

whereas, problems perceived to a less extent by nearly 20 percent of the development practitioners were:

- People's indifferent attitude towards development work.
- Too much of caste and class consciousness in the society.

With reference to the staff related problems, less than 40 percent of the development practitioners perceived the following problems to a great extent:

- Development practitioners' lack of motivation to continue in development work.
- Lack of trained professionals for development work.
- No freedom or autonomy to take decision.
- Lack of other privileges and benefits for the development practitioners.

whereas, same percentage of the development practitioners perceived the following problems to a less extent:

- Lack of readiness to travel for field work.
- Inconvenient working hours for staff members.
- Intellectual vacuum over a period of time in the organisation.
- Lack of modern management systems at workplace.

The table also shows that resources related problems were perceived to a great extent by nearly 20 percent of the development practitioners. They were:

- Lack of transportation for shifting beneficiaries to participate in development programmes.
- Inadequate number of equipments for development work such as TV, OHP, white boards and other materials.

The other problems like more time consumption in administrative/finance than programmatic, political interference in development work and lack of participation of people in development programmes were perceived by nearly 40 percent of the development practitioners to a great extent.

5.1.6 Challenges Development Practitioners face in Development Work

Table 19 reveals that the item-wise intensity indices for the perceptions of the development practitioners regarding the challenges they face in doing development work ranged from 2.44 to 2.14, i.e., all the challenges were faced to some extent only.

The highest intensity index was found to be 2.44 for a challenge in bringing desirable change in the lives of the people which means that the development practitioners faced this challenge in development work to some extent.

The development practitioners perceived other challenges like working with people, fund raising and utilising optimum resources and planning better programmes and approaches also to some extent only.

Table 19

Percentages and Item-Wise Intensity Indices Showing Perceptions Regarding Challenges that Development Practitioners face in doing Development Work

N = 80

Sr. No.	*Challenges*	*GE (%)*	*SE (%)*	*LE (%)*	*I.I.*
1.	Improving people's health status, educational status, living condition, etc.	51.25	41.25	7.50	2.44
2.	Encouraging more women to take benefits of development programme.	50.00	40.00	10.00	2.40
3.	Encouraging people to participate in planning, organising, implementing programme. 47.50	41.25	11.25	2.38	
4.	Collecting funds for development programmes.	43.75	46.25	10.00	2.34
5.	Working with the downtrodden groups51.25	30.00	18.75	2.33	

(Contd...)

(Contd...)

6. Planning need-based programmes such as HIV/AIDS awareness, immunisation, literacy, etc.	51.25	30.00	18.75	2.33
7. Developing better approach for a successful programme.	45.00	40.00	15.00	2.30
8. Utilising resources like human, raw materials at optimum level	36.25	51.25	12.50	2.24
9. Working in harsh conditions such as climatic changes rains and natural calamities.	37.50	42.50	20.00	2.17
10. Using strategies involving various media such as fold, multimedia, radio, and TV graphics, etc.	38.75	36.25	25.00	2.14

Percentage-wise the table shows that the following challenges were perceived to a great extent by almost 50 percent of the development practitioners:

- Working with people and bringing a desirable change in their lives.
- Encouraging women to take benefits of development programmes.
- Planning need based programmes for the people.
- Encouraging people to participate in development programmes at various stages.

whereas less than one-fourth of the development practitioners perceived the following challenges to a less extent:

- Developing a better approach for a successful programme.
- Utilising resources optimally for an effective programme.
- Working in harsh conditions.
- Using innovative communication strategies involving various media.

5.2 Variable-wise Overall Differences in Perceptions of Development Practitioners Regarding Their Problems

Table 20

Variable-wise Difference in Perceptions of Development Practitioners Regarding Overall Problems

N = *80*

Sr. No.	*Variables*	*N*	*Mean*	*S. D.*	*t – value*
1.	Age				
	– Younger	50	78.02	11.64	-1.12
	– Older	30	81.27	13.97	NS
2.	Sex				
	– Male	44	77.50	12.54	-1.36
	– Female	36	81.33	12.46	NS
3.	Educational qualification				
	– Average	26	80.15	13.07	0.45
	– High	54	78.80	12.43	NS

NS = Not Significant at 0.05 level with df = 78 t-tab = 1.65

Table 21.

Variable-wise Summary of ANOVA for Difference in Perceptions of Development Practitioners Regarding Overall Problems

N = *80*

Sr. No.	*Variables*	*Source*	*Sum of Squares*	*Mean Squares*	*F - value*
1.	Type of development organisation	Between groups	409.90	204.92	1.35 NS
		Within groups	11535.77	151.79	
2.	Length of experience in development work	Between groups	436.78	218.39	1.40 NS
		Within groups	12055.71	156.57	

NS = Not Significant at 0.05 level with f-tab = 2.99

Tables 20 and 21 shows that there was no significant difference in the perceptions of the development practitioners regarding the problems they face while doing development work in relation to their age, sex, educational qualification, type of development organisation and length of experience in development work.

It means that age, sex, educational qualification, type of development organisation and length of experience in development work of the development practitioners did not make any significant difference in the perceptions of development practitioners regarding the problems they face while doing development work.

Thus, the null hypothesis stating that there will be no significant differences in the overall perceptions of the development practitioners regarding the problems in relation to age, sex, educational qualification, type of development organisation and length of experience in development work was accepted.

5.3 Communication Strategies used by Development Practitioners while Conducting Development Work

The open ended question on the communication strategies used while conducting development work was responded by 54 development practitioners so N for this table was 54.

Table 22 reveals that majority of the development practitioners used two way communication or one- to- one interaction, meeting and IEC materials for conducting development work. Nearly half of the development practitioners used folk media, participatory rural appraisal and film shows for conducting development programmes. Less than 20 percent of the development practitioners used training, games, local leaders and local language, focused group discussions, exposure visit, exhibition and radio and TV programmes for conducting development work followed by less than 10 percent of the development practitioners using home visits, counselling, puppet shows, press releases, mass awareness programmes, workshops, seminars, public demonstration, positive experience sharing and *shibir* for development work.

5.4 Indicators used by Development Practitioners to Measure Outcome of Development Work

The open-ended question on indicators used to measure outcome of development work was responded by 55 development practitioners so N for this table was 55.

Table 22

Percentage Distribution of Development Practitioners According to Communication Strategies used for Development Work

N = 54

Sr. No.	*Communication Strategies*	*Percentage*
1.	Two way communication	79.62
2.	Meetings	66.67
3.	Information Education Communication (IEC) materials	48.15
4.	Folk media	47.25
5.	Participatory Rural Appraisal (PRA)	46.33
6.	Film shows	44.00
7.	Training	18.52
8.	Games	14.81
9.	Local leaders	12.96
10.	Focused group discussions	12.96
11.	Exposure visit	12.96
12.	Exhibitions	11.11
13.	Radio and TV programmes	11.11
14.	Home visits	9.26
15.	Counselling	5.56
16.	Mass awareness programmes	5.56
17.	Puppet shows	3.70
18.	Press releases	3.70
19.	Workshops / demonstrations / seminars	3.70
20.	Positive experience sharing	3.70
21.	*Shibir*	1.85

Table 23

Percentage Distribution of Development Practitioners according to Indicators used to Measure Outcome of Development Work

N = 55

Sr. No.	*Indicators*	*Percentage*
1.	Involvement and participation of community in development programmes	25.00
2.	Development of community based organisations by community itself	25.00
3.	Change in qualitative life style of the people	25.00
4.	Change in affective domain	
	– Change in behaviour pattern of people	25.58
	– Change in thinking pattern of people	24.00
	– Change in attitudes of people	22.50
	– Change in skills of people	21.25
	– Change in knowledge of people	21.52
5.	Health status	
	– Improved health and nutrition	23.75
	– Infant mortality rate	4.65
	– Maternal mortality rate	4.65
	– Number of anaemic people	3.55
	– Number of institutional deliveries	3.25
	– Improved disease prevalence	2.00
6.	Improved education and literacy	20.00
7.	Gender equality and empowerment	
	– Participation of women in development programmes	20.55
	– Women making decisions	19.75
8.	Income of the people	
	– Change in distribution pattern of income on expenses	19.25
	– Change in consumption pattern	17.50
	– Reduction of poverty and hunger	17.50
9.	Water management	
	– Sustainable water supply	6.50
	– Availability of drinking water	5.55
	– Cleanliness and sanitation	5.50

(Contd...)

(Contd...)

10.	Demand generation of people	4.25
11.	Awareness amongst the target group about various issues4.00	
12.	Improved infrastructure	4.00
13.	Improved agriculture	3.75
14.	Environmental sustainability	3.55

To measure the change in affective domain, nearly one-fourth of the development practitioners used change in behaviour pattern as an indicator followed by little more than 20 percent of the development practitioners using change in skills, knowledge, thinking pattern and attitudes as an indicator to measure the change in affective domain.

Involvement and participation of community in development programmes, development of community based organisations by community's support and change in qualitative lifestyle of the people were used as indicators to measure development work by nearly 25 percent of the development practitioners. Nearly one-fourth of the development practitioners used improved health and nutrition as an indicator to measure health status followed by nearly five percent of the development practitioners using infant mortality rate, maternal mortality rates, number of anaemic people, number of institutional deliveries and improved disease prevalence as an indicator to measure the development work. Nearly 20 percent of the development practitioners used improved education and literacy rate as an indicator to measure education, participation of women and decision making to measure gender equality and empowerment and change in pattern of distribution of income on expenses, change in consumption pattern and reduction of poverty and hunger as an indicator to measure the income of the people.

Very few percentages of the development practitioners used the following indicators:

- Sustainable water supply, availability of drinking water, cleanliness and sanitation for measuring water management
- Demand generation of people

- Awareness amongst the target group
- Improved infrastructure
- Improved agriculture
- Environmental sustainability.

Table 24

Percentage Distribution of Development Practitioners According to Motivating Sources to join Development Sector

N = 55

Sr. No.	*Motivating Sources*	*Percentage*
1.	Self-motivation	47.45
2.	Sensitisation towards the underprivileged section and an opportunity to work for them	34.55
3.	Education qualification	16.36
4.	Satisfaction to work for the weaker sections of the society	16.36
5.	Family and friends	9.09
6.	Training	7.27
7.	Approach towards development work	3.64

5.5 Motivation of Development Practitioners to join Development Sector

The open ended question on the motivating sources to join development sector was responded by 55 development practitioners so N for this table was 55.

Nearly 50 percent of the development practitioners were self-motivated to join the development sector followed by 35 percent of the development practitioners motivated due to sensitisation towards the underprivileged section and an opportunity to work for them. Less than 20 percent of the development practitioners were motivated through their formal education and a feeling of satisfaction to work for the weaker sections of the society to join the development sector. Less than 10 percent of the development practitioners were motivated by family and friends, training, the approach towards development work.

6

Discussions

The chapter presents a discussion of the findings of the study and their implications.

6.1 Profile of the Development Practitioners

6.1.1. Variable-wise

The findings of the present study revealed that a majority of the development practitioners were young in age, males, had high educational qualification, belonged to non-government organisation and had less experience in development work.

The findings of the study revealed that the development practitioners were young in age. The field of development practice is emerging as a new avenue for study and career. Earlier emphasis was on increase in Gross Development Product (GDP) and Gross National Product (GNP) for measuring development status but for last few decades there is a paradigm shift and emphasis is put on Human Development Index (HDI) to measure development. With emphasis on HDI, the development sector is emerging stronger all over the world. It is now emerging as a profession and discipline of study. The development practitioners are required to have relevant knowledge, understanding and a professional approach to their work. Special courses are offered to enhance the capabilities of the individuals to meet the demands of the development sector. Earlier it did not enjoy a status of profession. Welfare activities were mainly carried out by the higher strata of the society and by the individuals who were interested in doing social work. As development work emerged as profession, importance is being given to the development practitioners and they are required to be specially educated, dedicated, and competent and committed to meet the needs of the development sector. There is rapid development taking place in various vistas, namely, technology, education, industrialisation but on the other hand evils of poverty, unemployment, illiteracy, child labour, gender bias, ill health are still prevalent in our country. To combat these evils international and national agencies, local level agencies, corporate, government and non-government organisations are getting involved in the development sector and recruiting trained development practitioners. Therefore, a majority of the development practitioners under the study might be young in age.

A majority of the development practitioners under the study were males. The nature of work for the development practitioners is very different from regular white collar or formal institutional jobs. They are required to work in rural and tribal areas for long hours, travel a lot and conduct more field based activities, which require more of physical strength. Women play multiple roles in the family. Men have lesser family responsibility. It is inconvenient for many trained females to continue with the development work as their dual role and responsibility do not allow them to do justice to either the family responsibility or professional work. Therefore, a majority of the development practitioners might be males.

The development practitioners under the study were highly qualified. Today development agencies are demanding post graduation as required qualification for development work. To meet the demands of the growing development sector, the abilities of decision making, planning, conducting grassroots level field work, analysing, reporting and documenting the work are very important and they are expected to be well developed with higher education. Higher education also inculcates awareness, knowledge, confidence, skills, values, preparedness for world of work and a broad vision to accelerate the pace of development. With specialised education, professional approach for one's work also develops. Therefore, most of the development organisations prefer post graduates. This might be the reason for the development practitioners having high level of education.

The findings of the study also showed that majority of the development practitioners belonged to non-government organisations. NGOs are full time dedicated to development work. Government organisations and corporate houses have taken up added responsibility of development work but they have other major responsibilities and targets to be achieved. NGOs are full-fledged working for the development of the society and they employ individuals for development work only. Individuals in NGOs are value driven, committed and self-motivated to identify and adopt appropriate approach towards their target group, engendering trust and enhancing authentic participation. Today various national and international funding is available to NGOs to carry out development work. They also develop collaboration and partnerships with government, academicians and corporate sectors to do the development work.

NGOs have been found successful in doing development work. They not only implement the programmes but also play a very supporting role in mobilising human and non-human resources. Government departments involved in administering development work and corporate sectors willing to take up social responsibility may not have development professionals or subject matter experts, and necessary experience and knowledge in working for various areas of development, for example, grassroots level. Most of the times, they are required to collaborate with NGOs to implement their social development projects. So NGOs play a key role in development process and this might be the reason that majority of the development practitioners belonged to NGOs.

The findings also revealed that majority of the development practitioners were less experienced in development work. The development sector is still growing and coming up as a promising and lucrative career. Development work in our country is being carried for hundreds of years and it is still going on. Development practice as a profession is a new concept that is emerging. The importance of development practice is highlighted educationally and professionally. The systematic academic training sensitises the development practitioners to work for the underprivileged sections of the society and they are thus motivated to apply their skills and knowledge to social cause rather than profit oriented ones. In last few years, people must have realised its importance as a profession and must have opted for it as their specialisation. Therefore, this might be the reason for majority of the development practitioners being less experienced.

6.1.2 Other Characteristics

The findings of the present study showed that majority of the development practitioners had specialised training for working as development practitioners.

As discussed earlier, development practitioners are important change agents of the society. Specialised training provides in-depth knowledge and clear understanding of the ground realities of the development process. This will help the development practitioners to perform better and speed up the development. Development practitioners trained for the job are used to hard work, so it is easier for them to adjust to the demands of this profession and thus give their 100 per cent to the work. They can better execute the programmes with better vision of development process. Specialised training background will create sensitivity towards the issue of development and the development practitioners can contribute to an ethical, professional and responsible workforce. Training can enhance the development of competencies required to carry out the development work. The development practitioners are better prepared to apply the concepts of flexibility, cooperation, and comfort with uncertainty to face unique challenges in their day-to-day development work. They would develop people-centred vision of development and act as facilitator bringing people together in order to do any development programme. They are able to bring innovativeness, creativity and grass root level approach to development practice.

Development sector is challenging in many ways, so trained professionals are essential to meet the challenges. Thus, development practice provides opportunities to create tremendous impact in the world of professional and organised philanthropy. Therefore, majority of the development practitioners under the study might have undergone specialised training for working as development practitioners.

The findings of the present study showed that high majority of the development practitioners had women and children as their target group. All through the ages, women on the basis of gender have always been discriminated in almost all the societies of the world. Gender inequality in India exists in terms of gross population, literacy, sex ratio, socioeconomic status and opportunities. Sex ratio has always been a matter of serious concern for India, as it has been gone lower than 900 females per thousands males for a long time. Women are the most vulnerable groups in our society. They perform multiple roles but their status is still low. The health status as well as literacy rate among women is low. They have no voice in the family. They are deprived of an equal access to health care, education and economic rights. They are in need of development programmes for increasing their awareness and knowledge level, health status, environmental conservation, and becoming empowered.

Children are also the vulnerable section of our society. They need special care and protection if the future of the nation is to be made secure. Children being the asset of the nation should be grown up to become robust, physically fit, mentally alert and morally healthy citizens. 'Child is the father of man' is an old, but true saying, because the conduct and character of an adult person reflects what he has imbibed in childhood. The interest of the child is the interest of the society and of the nation at large. Hence, women and children have been the target groups of majority of the development practitioners.

The findings of the study also revealed that majority of the development practitioners were involved in report writing and documentation work in the organisation apart from planning, implementing, supervising and evaluating development programmes. Development practice requires dealing with variety of roles and responsibilities. As human beings are involved in the development programmes, one cannot be dealing with them mechanically. The word 'development' is debated many a times and new concepts and areas keep emerging. Lot of knowledge is being generated on development. A wide range of activities and programmes are also conducted in the development sector. So a systematic documentation of the knowledge and information on development and the activities is essential.

Today government funding agencies demand reports of the development work funded by them. The report gives authenticity to the work carried out by the organisation. Information on development strategy is also disseminated through the reports. Dissemination of the report also gives status to the organisation and guidelines to the other agencies for their development work planning in future. Earlier, documentation of development work was not done systematically and professionally, so it could not be utilised for giving direction and shape to future development work. Ever since human development became an important criterion in measuring the development index of any country, documentation of the development work carried out has become a necessity for every development organisation. Therefore, these days in recruiting the development practitioners the agencies are selecting post graduate candidates with documentation skills. Therefore, a majority of the development practitioners must have been involved in report writing and documentation apart from planning, implementing, supervising and evaluating development programmes.

The findings of the study also showed that majority of the development practitioners worked in rural areas, whereas, only four percent of the development practitioners worked in the areas like coastal, arid zone, forest and so on. Rural areas are still a priority for development work. The problems of illiteracy, poverty, unemployment, population, health disorders are found amongst the rural as well as the weaker sections of the society. The rural sector occupies an important place in India's economy. About 74 per cent of India's population lives in its 5,80,000 or so villages. Rural sector forms the basic foundation of India's economy. Despite the impressive progress that India has made since Independence, the rural sector and people remain grossly underdeveloped with about 55 per cent of the rural people being illiterate and 37 per cent of India's population living below the poverty line in 1993–94 (Singh, 1999: 35).

Agriculture is the main occupation in the rural areas. But agriculture and other allied activities contribute very less to India's gross domestic product. Therefore, rural people are poor. People in rural areas are not able to meet their minimum requirement of food, clothing and shelter. The villages miserably lack basic infrastructure such as schools, health care centres, drinking water facilities, electricity for domestic and agricultural purposes and means of transport and communication. The rural people are still traditional and superstitious in nature. They are illiterate, unemployed, have health disorders. Due to all these problems, maximum development work is carried in rural areas.

Singh (1999) pointed out that there is a need for the government to accord a very high priority, next only to defence, to rural development and to formulate a comprehensive national rural development policy, guaranteeing a reasonably satisfactory level of living to everyone in the sector, and liberating them from their servitude to ignorance, the rich, the elite and nature. Thus, majority of the development practitioners are working in rural areas.

Today, due the migration and other social problems, weaker sections are located in urban areas also. They have their specific development needs. They also should be considered for development. India also has a good coastal line and vast forest areas. With fast growing population, coastal and forest areas are coming up as the areas requiring development inputs.

6.2 Perceptions of the Development Practitioners on the Selected Aspects of Development

6.2.1. Meanings Attached to Development

The findings of the study revealed that the development practitioners perceived development as building up an enabling environment for people to enjoy long, healthy and creative life, fulfilling basic needs of the people, inculcating positive attitudes and values amongst people, providing opportunity to every individual to grow and reach their full potentials, developing and improving educational institutions, preparing and organising people for development to a great extent.

Today human beings are at the centre of development activities. People are regarded as the means and ends of development. The concept of human development and sustainable development is emphasized in development planning nowadays, so this might have led the development practitioners to perceive development as people's development.

Fulfilling the basic needs of the people is necessary. Rapid changes are taking place in our country, but still basic needs of food, shelter, nutrition, health, education, employment, etc. of the weaker sections are not fulfilled. People are the wealth of our country. How can a country be said as developed nation if the people of the country are not happy and satisfied or when their minimum basic requirements are not fulfilled. The quality of life of the people is consiι.ered as an important indicator in measuring the outcome of development. If the people's minimum needs are not achieved, how can they live a good quality contended life? Basic needs are very important for the people to live a life with minimum needs. Therefore, the development practitioners might have perceived the meanings of development as fulfilling the basic needs of the people to a great extent.

6.2.2 Priority Areas of Concern for Development

The findings of the study revealed that literacy, health education, poverty alleviation, gender empowerment, water and sanitation were perceived as the priority areas of high concern for development by the development practitioners.

After Independence, India has made remarkable progress in the fields of science and technology, and it is now self-sufficient in food grains and milk production. India has not yet been able to fully develop and harness its human and natural resources for the benefit of its people, and it has yet to solve its pernicious problems of illiteracy, poverty, unemployment and vulnerability to natural calamity (Singh, 1999). The national development planning also prioritises to solve the problems of illiteracy, health, poverty, water scarcity, gender inequality. Therefore these issues have always remained priority concerns for the development project planners.

Apart from keeping national development goals in focus, development practitioners have the freedom to set their own directions. They are close to the people at grassroots level, so they can very well understand the problems and issues of the people. They have the chance to identify and define the problems and issues they want to address. They are key players in the development of the nation. They are directly involved with the people at grassroots level, so they have an opportunity to develop innovative and creative solutions to development issues.

In spite of rapid development taking place in many areas, illiteracy is still a problem in our country. Illiteracy in India has, been regarded as an obstacle to development. The literacy rate in India in different years was found as: 1901: 5.3 per cent, 1921: 7.2 per cent, 1941: 16.1 per cent, 1961: 24.0 per cent, 1981: 36.2 per cent and 1991: 52.1 per cent (Ahuja, 1997). The latest census report (2001) reveals that at the beginning of new millennium literacy rate in India stands at 65.38 per cent. Seeing these low rates, literacy has remained the centre for development projects.

For decades, literacy has always been one of the major components of our development programmes as literacy brings awareness, knowledge, employment and good health. These are basic to the development of a nation. It is commonly believed that without substantially eliminating illiteracy, India cannot become a cohesive nation and give to all its citizens the quality of life they have long yearned for.

Zaveri (1996) states that development cannot be imposed or thrust upon people who are not prepared to accept change. Literacy is a change agent. Literacy is vital for people to go ahead and progress. It is the basis for the development of the masses in a democratic nation like India. Therefore literacy might be the priority area of high concern for development programmes.

Health does not mean survival only, it concerns physical, mental, economic and social well being of an individual as well. An investment in health not only improves the quality of life, but it is also a part of human resource development, which in turn affects various sectors of national economy. Health is man's greatest possession, for it lays a solid foundation for his happiness. It is a pre-requisite to human productivity and the 'development' process.

Enhancing the quality of growth is an important objective of the development paradigm in many developing countries. Better health, education, equal and wider job opportunities to all, trustworthy and transparent people's institutions, sustainable and cleaner environment, dignity, self-esteem and life security, among others, are key manifestations of the quality of growth (World Bank 2000).

The progress of the society greatly depends on the quality of its people. But the health status of the people in the country is low.

It needs to be enhanced. The people suffer from many health problems. A wide range of activities are covered under health, such as population control, family welfare, prevention of food adulteration, drug control, immunisation and eradication of major communicable and non-communicable diseases, as health concerns. Today development of the country is measured through HDI and GDI. The poor health status of our people is bringing down our HDI and GDI, so more emphasis is put on improving the health of the people. Health education should be provided to the people. Through health education, people will come to know about various health disorders, their prevention and cure. Therefore, health must have been perceived as one of the most concerned areas for development practitioners.

Poverty alleviation is also a major focus of all development programmes. Poverty is one of the most important problems that India is facing today. India ranks nineteenth in world industrial production and twelfth in total gross national production, yet it has a large population living below poverty line. National income is a comprehensive index of the sate of nation's economy and a measure of its growth over time. The figures of national income in India available for the last four decades do record some rise. National income in 1950-51 increased by 1.47 per cent in 1980-81 increased by 2.23 per cent and by 5.1 per cent in 1995-96. But the increase in the growth rate in comparison to other development countries is very low. People face other problems due to poverty. Hence poverty alleviation is a major concern for all development programmes.

Women form an integral part of the society. Women in the Indian society have been victims of humiliation, torture and exploitation. But today, they are being gradually recognised as important, powerful and meaningful contributors to the life of men; but till a few decades back, their condition was pitiable. Women are the focus of all development. For any sustainable change towards progress needs involvement of women. They perform multiple roles in the family and the society. Still their status is secondary. In spite of their contribution there is lot of gender discrimination and inequality existing in the society. Gender empowerment focuses on gender inequality in economic and political opportunities and participation in decision making process and values. The equality varies from community to community, race to race and region to region within a particular country. Indian economy has grown faster, but our population growth has neutralised this growth to a large extent. In the context of gender related development, it is disheartening that the enrolment, participation and literacy rate of girls as compared to boys have not been sought. Even the millennium development goals (MDGs) focus on improving the health of the people and gender equality among the masses.

India is very well endowed with water resources. With an average annual rainfall of about 120 cm in the country, and surface flow of about 188 million hectares metres, India has vast water resources. However, the total utilisable water is 114 million hectares metres. Despite of vast water resource, people do not have access to water for irrigation, safe drinking water.

Water is an inexhaustible gift of nature. However, its uneven distribution in space and time has often threatened human welfare, livelihood and economic development. The growing scarcity of water has been the result of rapidly growing population, rising demand for food and cash crops, increasing urbanisation and rising standard of living. Drinking water supply and sanitation are the basic needs of life. In spite of the concerted efforts made for increasing drinking water facilities, there have been yawning gaps between demand and supply of water. Water is a resource that belongs to the community. In view of the limited water available and, that too, unevenly and polluted, there is a need to adopt some conservation measuring for balanced and adequate supply of water to various users.

The above-mentioned might be the reasons for perceiving literacy, health education, poverty alleviation, gender empowerment, water and sanitation as priority areas of high concern by the development practitioners.

6.2.3 Competencies Required by Development Practitioners

The findings of the study showed that the development practitioners perceived competencies like communication skills, ability to lead the group and work with the team, problem-solving ability, confidence in carrying out development work, ability to judge the situation for immediate action, tactful handling of critical situation in development work, futuristic vision and ability to take initiative for development work to be required to a great extent.

As discussed earlier the development practitioners play a vital role in development practice. They plan, organise, implement, supervise and evaluate programmes and guide to people to achieve goals. The goal of the development practitioners is to make life of people better and satisfying. For changing the lives of the people, the development practitioners are required to be very competent. Development is a challenging field. To survive in this competitive world, competency is the prerequisite. It is not easy to work with people. If the development practitioners are highly competent, they can work in a better way and meet the problems and challenges easily.

Communication skills were perceived to be required by the development practitioners to a great extent. Communication is an essential requirement of human life. We are living in the world, where communication skills are very important. The development practitioners are the change agents for the people at grassroots level. They are the liaison between people at grassroots level and the policy and programme planners. So communication skills are most important for the development practitioners. People have established thoughts, tradition, customs, beliefs, and so on. To change these thoughts, traditions for better living requires excellent communication skills. It is necessary for the development practitioners to persuade and convince people for desirable change. People will not accept new ideas and concepts easily. The development practitioners are also required to collect funds for development programmes. It is not an easy task; they have to work a lot on the plans and procedures. To convince the funding agencies, communication skills play a vital role. This might be the reason for the development practitioners perceiving communication skills as a competency for development work to a great extent.

Problems-solving ability, the ability to judge the situation for immediate action and tactful handling of critical situations in development work were the competencies perceived to be required by the development practitioners to a great extent. Development work is a tough task. There are problems that arise with the target group, in the development process, while collecting funds, and so on. The development practitioners should have good problem solving ability. They should be able to analyse problems, find their root causes and alternative solutions. Variety of problems arises while working on field and need immediate action. So the ability of judging situations and decision for actions is necessary.

6.2.4 Approaches to be used as a Basis for Planning Development Programmes

The findings of the study revealed that participatory approach, development support communication approach and localised approach were perceived to a great extent as a basis for planning development programmes by the development practitioners.

Our country is modernising at a rate faster than it can cope with, so result oriented approach is sought. With emphasis on Gross Domestic Product (GDP) along with Human Development Index (HDI), human development is emphasised along with economic development in planning development strategy at national level. Thus, human development through modernisation approach has remained in the centre of all development planning.

Participatory approach focuses on participation of people at different stages like planning, implementing, supervising and evaluating development work. Participation means bringing people into action to achieve the set goals. It also means empowerment of people to work towards achievement of the goals of development. People directly benefit by participation in development programmes. They get empowered and their overall personality also enhances.

Participation leads to people's development where people plan, execute and judge the effectiveness of the programmes. All development programmes insist participatory approach as participation helps in preparing and executing effective development plans by assessing felt needs of the people. It also protects the people from deprivation, subjugation and exploitation by others and empowers them by developing skills and abilities to manage situations in a better way. Participation is an important event that emphasises the quality of life of local societies as a step towards the realisation of self–reliant, sustainable development and social justice. Participation is considered as an essential ingredient for sustainable development programmes by international and multilateral agencies. The funding agencies today prefer to fund the projects which are participatory in nature.

India has been a crucible of various languages, cultures, religions, climates, resources, infrastructure, and so on. So depending on the specific requirement of the project, the approach should be decided. Localised approach focuses on meeting the local needs of the people with the help of local resources. This facilitates two way communication by allowing greater involvement and participation of the people in the development programmes. It encourages the people and communities to become more aware about their needs and resource availability. It helps people to develop and restore the sense of belonging to a local community where people are interested in working together for their own development, or towards a common goal of sustainable development.

Development support communication approach is based on participatory approach focusing on basic needs and knowledge sharing on co-equal basis. It focuses on participation using small media that are accessible and appropriate for the community. Depending on the project requirement, development support communication approach emphasizes on supportive use of media. This approach is also being applied widely by development practitioners nowadays.

Top-down, linear and diffusion of innovation approaches were used earlier, but due to certain drawbacks of these approaches their importance has gone down. They failed to create a positive impact in changing the lives of the people. In today's era where development is a dire need, participatory, localised and development support communication approaches are widely used.

Therefore, majority of the development practitioners might have perceived participatory approach, localised approach and development support communication approach as a basis for planning development programmes to a great extent.

6.2.5 Problems faced by Development Practitioners

The findings of the study showed that the problems like existence of poverty and illiteracy, lack of job security for the development practitioners, people's indifferent attitude towards development work, people's lack of awareness about development programmes and local leader's dominance in development work were perceived to some extent by the development practitioners.

The findings also showed that there were no significant differences in the perceptions of the development practitioners regarding the problems in development work in relation to their age, sex, educational qualification, type of development organisation and length of experience in development work. It means that irrespective of age, sex, educational qualification and type of development organisation and length of experience in development, all the development practitioners faced more or less the similar problems. Development work involves dealing with social issues and human beings – their mind sets, attitudes, practices which pose challenges and problems to the development practitioners.

This could mean that the development practitioners are well oriented about the ground realities in the development sector and well prepared to tackle the problems. The development agencies must also have prepared and oriented them about the situation. They are well trained to face problems and solve them. As discussed earlier, they were trained for working in the development organisation. The training might have induced indepth knowledge and clear understanding of development work. The kind of training provided to the development practitioners is very effective and appropriate. So they are well prepared to work with the people in harsh conditions which lead to lesser problems.

Existence of poverty and illiteracy is a problem perceived by the development practitioners to some extent. The vicious circle of poverty rules our country. All the problems like poverty, illiteracy, unemployment, gender discrimination, etc. are interlinked. People are dying of hunger, diseases and disorders and poverty. This is a major problem since years. Massive development programmes are taken up, but the problem of poverty and illiteracy is not yet solved. Due to poverty and illiteracy, people are not able to take optimum benefits of the development programmes. They are not able to fulfil their needs.

People understand the importance of health, income generation, population and environment but are not able to practice it in their day to day lives due to poverty and illiteracy. This might be the reason for the development practitioners to perceive existence of poverty and illiteracy as problems in the society faced to some extent.

People's lack of awareness about development programmes and their indifferent attitude towards development work were also perceived as problems faced to some extent by the development practitioners. People have not realised the importance of development programmes and they think it as a waste of time participating in. People do not attend the programmes which are specifically designed for them. They are not even aware of some development programmes, so they are unable to take benefits of the programme. The main objective of the development programmes is development of the weaker sections of the society, but due to people's indifferent attitude and lack of awareness about development programmes, the programmes fail to achieve the objectives.

6.2.6 Challenges faced by Development Practitioners

The findings of the study showed that the challenges like working with down trodden people and bringing about a change in their lives, fund raising through optimum resources utilisation, planning better programmes and approaches were perceived as challenges in development work to some extent by the development practitioners.

When problems are there challenges always follow while dealing with various agencies, heterogeneous groups, varying resources and field work in development sector, challenges are ought to be there. It is interesting to find that the stated challenges are perceived to be faced by the development practitioners to some extent. It is a positive trend for the development sector. This shows that the development practitioners are more competent, well-trained and exposed to the grassroots situations adequately. As discussed earlier, specially trained and highly qualified development practitioners have indepth knowledge and clear understanding of the development process. Another possible reason could be that, when the target groups are convinced and willing to participate in the development programmes. The people are willing to take optimum advantage of the help provided by the development practitioners. However, the development practitioners would face the challenge of meeting the expectations of the enlightened target group.

6.3 Communication Strategies used for Conducting Development Work

The findings of the study also revealed that high majority of the development practitioners used two way communication and meetings for conducting development work, whereas, nearly 50 per cent of the development practitioners used IEC material, folk media, PRA for development work, followed by less than 10 per cent of the development practitioners using home visits, counselling, puppet shows, positive experience sharing, mass awareness programmes and workshops and seminars.

Communication has attained a great importance in the development programmes. It is the foundation upon which development planners builds various programmes for attaining the goals of economic and social advancement of the society. It serves as the most vital means in convincing people for the acceptance and adoption of innovations. The useful development messages are conveyed to the people by using different communication strategies to help them acquire new knowledge and habits required for coping with the fast changing society (Joshi, 2001:105).

A high majority of the development practitioners used two way communication and meetings for conducting development work. In two way communication, the development practitioners and people come together and discuss about the process of development programmes. Here the meetings or sessions become interactive. The people also participate in conducting different activities and decision making.

6.4 Indicators used to Measure the Outcome of Development Work

The findings of the study showed that nearly 25 per cent of the development practitioners used involvement and participation of community in development programmes as an indicator to measure development work, followed by one-fourth of the development practitioners using change in behaviour as an indicator to measure development work.

Evaluation is mostly defined as a more thorough examination than monitoring, at specified points is time, of programmes, projects or organisational performance, usually with emphasis on impact for people and commonly also relevance, effectiveness, efficiency, sustainability and replicability (Dale, 2004).

Measurement of development work is very much essential. It gives an idea that to what extent the planned outputs, expected changes, intended effects have been achieved. The overall consequences of the programmes for the intended beneficiaries can be known. It also helps to know where the development of the nation has reached so far. The effectiveness of the communication strategies used and the overall programme can be known.

Involvement and participation of the community in development programme was used as an indicator to measure development work by nearly 25 percent of the development practitioners. People as such do not attend development programmes. The development programmes are organised for the weaker sections but their priority is doing household work, earning money, etc., rather than attending the programmes taking benefit of it. Sometimes people take these programmes very lightly. They sometimes attend the programmes just for the sake of attending it. The development practitioners work hard to plan programmes for them and they try to collect more and more people as it is the people's programme. When people start taking interest and participate in the programmes at various levels, the programmes becomes fruitful. Involvement and participation of the people is must in development programme. It is their programme, so they should be involved to benefit out of it. This also means that people are now interested in development programmes and they really want to take the benefits of the development programmes. This might be the reason for using involvement and participation of community in development programmes as indicators to measure development work by the development practitioners.

The findings also showed that change in behaviour pattern was used as an indicator for measuring the outcome of development work by the development practitioners. Development programmes are designed for bringing a desirable change in the behaviour, knowledge, skills of the people. If the development programme helps to bring a desirable change in the behaviour pattern of the people, it is a positive development. People have their established traditions, attitudes and behaviour. But when planned behavioural change is observed, it means development is taking place. It leads to enhancement of the quality of life of the people. Thus, the development practitioners might have used change in behaviour pattern as an indicator to measure development work.

Indicators are developed theoretically, in standardised forms, but rarely usable in these forms. They require many technicalities, facilities and skills in their use. They are time consuming and fund involving. Many a times, it requires knowledge of economic, statistics, mathematics, conversions of various data and so on. So very practical and appropriate indicators should be developed and planned for better results.

6.5 Motivating Sources for Development Practitioners for joining Development Sector

The findings of the study showed that nearly 50 percent of the development practitioners were self motivated to join the development sector, whereas, nearly 35 percent of the development practitioners were motivated due to sensitisation towards the underprivileged sections and an opportunity to work for them.

The importance of development sector is increasing at a faster rate. The development practitioners might have realised the importance of development practice as a career opportunity as it is an emerging field. They may be motivated by the belief that their skills are best used to help overcome a wide range of critical social problems. Development practitioners might have seen the pitiable condition of the weaker sections of the society and are sensitised for their upliftment.

6.5.1. Implications of the Study for Development Agencies

1. The meaning of development as enlarging people's choices, participatory process of social change and conserving the environment for future generation should be strengthened among the development practitioners.
2. The areas like natural resource management, waste management, child labour, women's rights should be focused in planning development projects.
3. The participatory, localised and development support communication approaches should be promoted in development programmes.
4. The training of development practitioners should emphasise on development of competencies among the development practitioners. The competencies like documentation skills, ability to resolve conflicts, flexibility to adjust to changes required in development, ability to monitor and evaluate development programmes should be induced in the training and orientation of development practitioners.
5. Apart from rural, urban, tribal areas, development work should be promoted in coastal, forest, arid areas also as part of the field training in development work as they are also emerging as having their specific development needs.
6. Besides women and children, elderly and youth also should be included as target groups as ageing is emerging as an area of study by itself and youth have their own specific development needs.
7. Training in development and use of appropriate and practical indicators of development should be given to the development practitioners.
8. Development agencies, non-government organisations should organise training and refresher course for the development practitioners from time to time so that the required competencies are enhanced continuously.
9. Research on development process, various aspects of development and development practitioners should be encouraged by development agencies.

10. As all development agencies want their development practitioners to have skills in report writing and documentation of the development process, rigorous training in these areas should be included in development management course.

6.5.2. Implications of the Study for Academicians

1. The development management course should provide opportunities to students to practice participatory approach; human development approach based development work so that they are able to meet the challenges in present-day development practice more competently.
2. Academic institutions training students in development management should reinforce the competencies like documentation skills, ability to resolve conflicts, flexibility to adjust to changes required in development, ability to monitor and evaluate development programmes as they have been perceived to be the important one by the development practitioners.

6.6 Conclusion

The findings of the present study revealed that the development practitioners held various meanings for development term. The perceptions such as development means building up an enabling environment for people to enjoy a long, healthy and creative life, fulfilling basic needs of people, improving people's lifestyles through better education, providing opportunity to every human being to grow and reach their full potentials were found to be held by majority of the development practitioners to a great extent. The areas like literacy, health, poverty alleviation, gender empowerment, water and sanitation were perceived as priority areas of most concern for development by the development practitioners. They perceived that the competencies like communication skills, ability to lead the group, ability to work with the team, problem solving ability, confidence in carrying out development work are required to a great extent.

It can be concluded that participatory approach, development support communication approach and localised approach were perceived to a great extent as a basis for planning development programmes by the development practitioners. The problems like existence of poverty and illiteracy in the society, lack of job security for the development practitioners, people's lack of awareness about development programmes and local leader's dominance in development work were perceived to be faced by the development practitioners to some extent. They perceived that the challenges like bringing a desirable change in the lives of the people, encouraging more women to take benefits of development programmes, collecting funds for development programmes, working with the downtrodden groups are faced by the development practitioners to some extent.

It is very encouraging and interesting to note that the development practitioners perceived the challenges and problems to some extent only. In spite of problems and challenges, the development sector is growing as a lucrative career opportunity and young people are opting it as career. Development practice is a diverse and complex field. Today many university graduates forgo the high pay and perks of the corporate world to work in a development sector which is also known as non-for-profit business, where the priority is helping people in need rather than earning big bucks. This shows that the future of development sector is bright with the development practitioners ready to take up challenges and face problems.

Bibliography

Ahuja, R. (1997), *Social Problems in India.* Second Edition, Jaipur, Rawat Publications.

Alavi, Hamasza and Teodar Shanin (eds.) (1982), *Introduction to the Sociology of 'Developing Societies'*, London: McMillan.

Blossom, S. (2000), *A study of Woman Social Work Professionals in different Fields,* Unpublished Dissertation (MSW) Faculty of Social Work, M.S. University of Baroda, Vadodara.

Census Report 2001.

Chowdhary, P. (1996), NGO's need both fire and ice, *Journal of Social Welfare,* V.1., No.3., pp. 9-12.

Ganesh, S. (1994), *Lectures In Mass Communication,* New Delhi, Indian Publishers.

Goel, S. and Dhaliwal, S. (2004), *Slum Improvement through Participatory Urban Based Community Structures,* New Delhi, Deep and Deep Publications Pvt. Ltd.

Goulet Denis, A. (1971), *The Guel Choice : A New Concept in the theory of Development,* 1st ed. New York.

Gupta, V.S. (1995), *Third Revolution in Indian Perspective,* New Delhi, Concept Publishing Company.

Iyer, V. (2004), *A study of the status of Urban Rehabilitation and its Impact on the Social Life of People in Kutch.* Unpublished Dissertation, (MSW) Faculty of Social Work, M.S. University of Baroda. Vadodara.

Joshi, U. (2001), *Understanding Development Communication,* New Delhi, Dominant Publishers and Distributors.

Kaul Anuradha (1990), Educational, *Economic and Social Impact of Voluntary training Agencies offering Income Generating Programmes for Low SES Women of Baroda,* Unpublished Dissertation (Ph.D.) Dept. of Ext. & Communication, M.S. University of Baroda, Vadodara.

Khamesra, N. (2003), *Opinions of the Mothers Regarding the Influence of Television, Advertisements on the Consumer Behaviour of their Children,* Unpublished Dissertation (M.Sc.), Faculty of Family and Community Sciences, M.S. University of Baroda. Vadodara.

Khilnani, S. (2007), Looking Back for Lessons, *India Today,* July 2nd.

Mukhopadhyay (2008), Social Enterpreneureship. *Times of India* (Ascent) 4th June, 08, p.1.

Ojha, S. (1995-96), A comparative study of Knowledge and Attitudes of Extension Functionaries of Selected states of India and Country of Bangladesh regarding Population Education and Developing / Modifying the curricula for Extension Functionaries of both the Countries, Unpublished Dissertation (Ph.D.), Faculty of Family and Community Sciences, M.S. University of Baroda, Vadodara.

Parmar, R. (1998), *Training in NGOs – HRD Sub-System,* Unpublished Dissertation (MSW), Faculty of Social Work, M.S. University of Baroda, Vadodara.

Paul, S. (2005), *Study of Voluntary Organisation's Contribution to Social Development,* Unpublished Dissertation (MSW), Faculty of Social Work, M.S. University of Baroda, Vadodara.

Pezeshki – Rad, G. and Zamani, N. (2005), *Information Seeking Behaviour of Iranian Extension Managers and Specialists,* Information Research, 10(3). http://informationr.net/ir/10-3/paper229.html

Philips, A. (1997), *A Study of Functionaries in Human Care Agencies in Indore,* Unpublished Dissertation (MSW), *Faculty of Social Work,* M.S. University of Baroda, Vadodara.

Prakash, G. (2007), Liberty with Death, *India Today,* July 2 2007, pp. 20,21.

Schramm Wilber (1964), *The Role of Information in National Development,* Paris, Stanford University Press.

Sen Sanchari 1995), *Voluntary Organisations and Women Development,* Unpublished Dissertation, (MSW), Faculty of Social Work, M.S. University of Baroda. Vadodara.

Sidhpura, Megha. (2005), *Opinions of the Beneficiaries of the Selected Non-Government Organisations Working for the Welfare of Women in Baroda,* Unpublished Dissertation (M.Sc.) Faculty of Family and Community Sciences, M.S. University of Baroda, Vadodara.

Simon, B. (2000), *A Study of Women Social Work Professionals in Different Fields,* Unpublished Dissertation (MSW), Faculty of Social Work, M.S. University of Baroda, Vadodara.

Singh, K. (1999), *Rural Development – Principles, Policies and Management,* New Delhi, Sage Publications.

Singharoy, D. K. (2001), *Social Development and the Empowerment of Marginalised Groups,* New Delhi, Sage Publications.

Todaro, Michel (1977), *Economic Development in the Third World: An Introduction to Problems and Policies in a Global Perspective,* New York, Longman.

Trivedi, S. (1998), *Development Theories, Tribals and Common Property Resources, Politics of Deforestation in India,* Unpublished Dissertation (MA) Dept. of Political Science, Faculty of Arts, M. S. University of Baroda, Vadodara.

Wang and Dissanayake (1984), *'Culture, Development and Change: Some Explorative Observations In Wang and Dissanyake* (eds.), Continuity and Change in Communication Systems, pp.3-20, New Jersey : Ablex

World Bank Report 1997.

World Bank Report, 2000.

World Development Report, 1997.

Zaveri, H. (1996), An Action Project to Reinforce Literacy Skills Under Post Literacy Campaign of Nagar Prathmik Shikshan Samiti, Baroda City, through the use of Games. Unpublished Dissertation, Faculty of Family and Community Sciences, M.S. University of Baroda, Vadodara.

Webliography

http://azadindia.org/social-issues/literacy-in-india.html

http://www.totalkm.com

http://www.window2india.com/cms/content/article11092007.jsp?aid=4746

http://informationr.net/ir/10-3/paper?29.html

http://www.up.ac.za/dspace/bitstream/2263/2555/1/Rwelamira_Poverty(2000).pdf

http://forums.joeuser.com/82367

Index